Voodoo for Beginners

A Guide to New Orleans Voodoo, Haitian Vodou, and Hoodoo

Your Free Gift
(only available for a limited time)

Thanks for getting this book! If you want to learn more about various spirituality topics, then join Mari Silva's community and get a free guided meditation MP3 for awakening your third eye. This guided meditation mp3 is designed to open and strengthen ones third eye so you can experience a higher state of consciousness. Simply visit the link below the image to get started.

https://spiritualityspot.com/meditation

Table of Contents

Introduction

The great Maya Angelou once said, *"The more you know of your history, the more liberated you are."* And that is precisely what this book aims to do; to enlighten you about Voodoo's fascinating history, rituals, and practices.

Whether you're a skeptic or a believer, this book is for you if you want to look into the story of Voodoo. From the vibrant streets of New Orleans to the mystical land of Haiti, Voodoo has captivated people's imaginations for centuries. But what exactly is Voodoo? Is it a religion, a culture, a way of life, or something else entirely? These questions will be explored through this book's pages, which will delve into the complex and multifaceted world of Voodoo.

But what sets this book apart from the others on the market? For one, it's written in simple English that's easy to grasp. You'll never find yourself feeling lost about what the concepts within this book are as it leads you through the labyrinthine world of Voodoo.

And that's not all – this book is tailor-made for beginners. You don't need any prior knowledge or experience with Voodoo to pick up this guide and start your journey. The complex and sometimes daunting world of Voodoo has been distilled to leave you with crystal-clear knowledge on the topic.

But this book doesn't just stop at theory. It is also chock-full of hands-on methods and instructions. You'll learn how to create your own Voodoo dolls, cast spells, and perform rituals passed down for generations. With the step-by-step guides, you can practice Voodoo in your home and experience its transformative power for yourself.

As the great detective Sherlock Holmes once said, "It is a capital mistake to theorize before one has data." So, reading this book will provide you with the data you need to fully appreciate and understand the world of Voodoo. Whether you're a curious beginner or a seasoned practitioner, this guide is bound to enrich your knowledge and deepen your understanding of this ancient and mysterious tradition. So, what are you waiting for? Turn the page and begin a journey through the fascinating world of Voodoo.

Chapter One: Understanding Voodoo and Hoodoo

As you delve into the historical and cultural evolution of Haitian Vodou, New Orleans Voodoo, and Hoodoo, you will find a complex web of beliefs and practices intertwined with the experiences of African descendants in the Americas. These practices emerged as a way to preserve and celebrate African spirituality, often in the face of oppressive forces seeking to erase it.

Haitian Vodou

Haitian Vodou is a complex and nuanced spiritual practice that emerged from the experiences of enslaved West Africans in Haiti. The practice is deeply rooted in the traditions of West African spirituality and was further shaped by the forced life of slavery and the resistance of enslaved Africans toward their oppressors. The practice of Vodou began with the arrival of enslaved Africans in Haiti in the 16th century. These individuals came from various West African regions, each with their own spiritual traditions and practices. However, they were all brought together under the brutal living standards of slavery, and these spiritual practices became a way to preserve the slaves' original culture and resist the wishes of their oppressors.

One of the central beliefs of Haitian Vodou is the idea of the Loa, or spirits, who are seen as intermediaries between humans and the divine. The Loa are believed to be able to communicate with the ancestors and offer protection and guidance to those who honor them. Many of the Loa in Haitian Vodou have roots in West African spiritual traditions. Still, they have evolved and been adapted over time to reflect the experiences of Haitians. The practice of Haitian Vodou also includes elements of Catholicism, the dominant religion of the French colonizers in Haiti. The enslaved Africans in Haiti were forced to convert to Catholicism. Still, they often found ways to incorporate their own spiritual practices into the religion. For example, they identified Catholic saints with the Loa and used Catholic symbols and rituals in their Vodou ceremonies.

One of the most important aspects of Haitian Vodou is the role of the priest or priestess, known as the houngan or mambo. These individuals are believed to have a special connection to the Loa. They are responsible for leading ceremonies and performing rituals. The houngan or mambo undergo a period of training and initiation, during which they learn the secrets of Vodou and the ways to communicate with the Loa. The practice of Haitian Vodou has faced persecution and suppression throughout history. The French colonizers in Haiti saw Vodou as threatening their authority and tried to suppress it by force. However, Vodou continued to be practiced in secret, and it played a significant role in the Haitian Revolution, which resulted in Haiti becoming the first black republic in the world.

After the Haitian Revolution, Vodou continued to be practiced in Haiti and spread to other parts of the world. However, it was still viewed with suspicion and fear by many. In the early 20th century, the American journalist William Seabrook authored a sensationalized book about Vodou called "The Magic Island," which perpetuated many negative stereotypes about the practice. Despite these challenges, Haitian Vodou has continued evolving and adapting. Today, it is practiced by millions of people around the world and has had a significant impact on art, music, and literature. Haitian Vodou continues to be a powerful force for spiritual healing and cultural preservation, and it serves as a reminder of the sheer strength of African descendants in the Americas.

New Orleans Voodoo

New Orleans Voodoo, also known as Louisiana Voodoo, is a unique blend of African and European religious and cultural practices and Native American influences. It has been shaped by the history of the city and the people who have called it home. New Orleans Voodoo has its roots in the transatlantic slave trade, which brought millions of Africans to the Americas. Many of these enslaved Africans were from the areas now known as Benin and Togo, where the religion of Vodun (or Voodoo) originated. These Africans were forced to work on plantations in Louisiana, where they were forbidden to practice their own religions. However, they found ways to blend their traditions with those of their captors, resulting in the unique form of Voodoo that is still practiced in New Orleans today.

A Louisiana voodoo altar.
Greg Willis, CC BY-SA 2.0 <https://creativecommons.org/licenses/by-sa/2.0>, via Wikimedia Commons https://commons.wikimedia.org/wiki/File:Voodoo_Altar_New_Orleans.jpg

In the late 18th and early 19th centuries, several free people of color in New Orleans began practicing Voodoo openly. These practitioners were often healers and spiritual leaders in their communities, and their influence grew rapidly. They preserved many aspects of the original Vodun religion, including using ritual objects and worshiping ancestral spirits. One of the most well-known figures in the history of New Orleans Voodoo is Marie Laveau. Born in 1801, Laveau was a free woman of color who became a renowned Voodoo priestess. She was known for her healing powers and her ability to communicate with spirits. Laveau was so influential that she was said to have the power to grant or deny favors from the city's politicians.

After the Civil War, the practice of Voodoo began to decline in New Orleans as many African Americans converted to Christianity. However, their religion never completely died out. In the early 20th century, many writers and artists became interested in Voodoo, which began appearing in popular culture. This led to a revival of interest in religion among African Americans, and it has continued to be practiced in New Orleans to this day.

One of the key features of New Orleans Voodoo is its emphasis on personal relationships with spirits. Practitioners believe that spirits can be called upon to help with all manner of problems, from health issues to financial troubles. They also believe in using charms, talismans, and spells to protect themselves and their loved ones from harm. Another important aspect of New Orleans Voodoo is using music and dance in ritual practices. Voodoo ceremonies often involve drumming and chanting. Participants may enter into a trance-like state as they communicate with the spirits.

In recent years, New Orleans Voodoo has faced criticism from some quarters for its association with negative stereotypes, such as the idea of the "Voodoo doll" as a tool for revenge. However, practitioners argue that these stereotypes are based on misunderstanding the religion and its practices. They point out that Voodoo is a deeply spiritual and personal religion and has played an important role in the culture of New Orleans. Its history is intertwined with the city's history, and its traditions have been passed down through generations of practitioners. Whether you are a believer or a skeptic, there is no denying the unique and enduring influence of New Orleans Voodoo on the culture and mythology of America.

Hoodoo

Hoodoo, or *conjure*, is a spiritual practice developed among African Americans in the Southern United States. Its roots can be traced back to West and Central African religious practices brought to America during the transatlantic slave trade. Hoodoo has a complex and varied history, influenced by the traditions of multiple African ethnic groups and Native American and European American folk magic. Because of this, it has developed into a distinct spiritual practice with a unique blend of beliefs, rituals, and practices.

The word "hoodoo" itself is believed to have originated from the term "hudu" or "joodoo," which was used to describe a West African religious practice. Over time, "hoodoo" became a catch-all term for various African American spiritual practices. During the antebellum period, many enslaved Africans were forbidden from practicing their traditional religions. As a result, they adapted their beliefs and practices to fit within the Christian framework imposed upon them by their masters. This led to the development of a form of hoodoo incorporating elements of Christianity, including using the Bible and Christian saints in spells and rituals.

After the Civil War, hoodoo continued to evolve and adapt to the changing social and cultural landscape of the South. It became popular among rural and urban African Americans, and its practices were often passed down through oral tradition within families and communities. Hoodoo practitioners, also known as rootworkers, often created and sold amulets, talismans, and other items believed to have magical properties. They would also perform spells and rituals for clients seeking protection, healing, love, or prosperity.

In addition to its African roots, the practices of Native Americans and Europeans have influenced hoodoo. For example, using herbs and roots in hoodoo can be traced back to the Native American practice of using medicinal plants for healing. Meanwhile, European folk magic, such as using astrology and numerology, has also been incorporated into hoodoo practices. In the early 20th century, hoodoo gained a reputation for being associated with evil or dark magic. This was largely due to negative portrayals in the media and the practice's association with African American culture, often demonized by mainstream society.

Despite this negative perception, hoodoo continued to thrive within African American communities. In the mid-20th century, hoodoo became increasingly popular among white practitioners, particularly in the context of the American folk music revival. This also led to a renewed interest in hoodoo among African Americans, and the practice experienced a revival during the Civil Rights Movement. Hoodoo remains a vibrant and evolving spiritual practice with practitioners worldwide. While many aspects of the practice have changed over time, its core beliefs and values remain rooted in the African American experience and culture. For hoodoo practitioners, freedom is found in the ability to connect with their ancestors, spirits, and the divine and create a better world for themselves and their communities.

All three practices, Haitian Vodou, New Orleans Voodoo, and Hoodoo, have faced persecution and misrepresentation throughout history. They were often viewed as dangerous and were suppressed by the authorities. However, they have endured and evolved, adapting to new circumstances and incorporating new influences. Today, they continue to be practiced by people worldwide who seek a connection to their ancestors, protection from the spirits, and healing for their communities. The evolution of these practices is a testament to the resilience of African spirituality and the importance of preserving cultural traditions. By learning about these practices and understanding their historical and cultural contexts, you can gain a deeper appreciation for the diversity and richness of African spiritual practices and the experiences of African descendants in the Americas.

Similarities and Differences

As you explore the world of Afro-Caribbean religions, it's important to understand the similarities and differences between three distinct practices: Haitian Vodou, New Orleans Voodoo, and Hoodoo. While they share a common history and ancestry, each has its unique identity and beliefs. First, the similarities. All three practices result from the cultural syncretism between African and European traditions that occurred during the transatlantic slave trade. They are all practiced in the Americas and are a blend of West African, Native American, and European spiritual beliefs. The practitioners of all three practices believe in the power of ancestor veneration, divination, and the use of natural elements to effect change in their lives. All three also recognize the importance of spirits, deities, and the unseen world. Haitian Vodou, New Orleans Voodoo, and Hoodoo all utilize herbs, roots, and other natural elements to make medicines, charms, and potions. Each practice also involves using talismans, amulets, and spiritual baths.

Now, what are the differences? Haitian Vodou is an Afro-Haitian religion that emerged in Haiti during the 18th century. New Orleans Voodoo is a form originally developed in the southern United States, particularly in New Orleans. It has its roots in Haitian Vodou but also incorporates elements of Catholicism and Native American spirituality. New Orleans Voodoo also involves ceremonies and rituals, but they are generally less formal than those of Haitian Vodou. It strongly emphasizes ancestor veneration and the use of talismans, such as gris-gris bags, to protect oneself from harm or bring good luck. Hoodoo practitioners often incorporate Christian elements into their practice, such as using psalms and prayers in their spells and rituals. They also place a great deal of emphasis on rootwork, which involves using herbs, minerals, and other natural elements to create charms and potions for various purposes.

Respect These Practices

To approach Voodoo and Hoodoo with the respect they deserve, it is important to recognize their spiritual significance and the cultural traditions that underpin them. This requires an openness to learning and a willingness to engage with the practices thoughtfully and respectfully. One important aspect of this is recognizing the importance of formal initiation in Voodoo and Hoodoo. Initiation is a process by which a person is formally welcomed into a community of practitioners and given access to that community's knowledge and spiritual practices.

In Voodoo, initiation typically involves undergoing a series of rituals and ceremonies, including offerings to the spirits and the performance of divination. The objective of initiation is to establish a relationship between the practitioner and the spirits and to gain a deeper understanding of the spiritual significance of Voodoo. Similarly, in Hoodoo, initiation involves passing knowledge and practices from generation to generation. This can involve learning from a family member or other experienced practitioner and may involve undergoing specific rituals or ceremonies to mark the transition into full membership in the Hoodoo community. Initiation is essential in both Voodoo and Hoodoo because it allows practitioners to fully engage with the spiritual significance of these practices and to understand the deeper meanings behind the rituals and ceremonies they perform.

Another important aspect of approaching Voodoo and Hoodoo respectfully is avoiding whitewashing or appropriating these practices. This means recognizing and honoring the cultural traditions that underpin them and not attempting to strip them of their African roots. For example, in the United States, white practitioners of Hoodoo and Voodoo have long been appropriating these practices and attempting to erase these African roots. This can take many forms, from claiming to have access to secret knowledge or spiritual powers to co-opting symbols and practices from other cultures and presenting them as their own. To avoid this kind of appropriation, it is important to approach Voodoo and

Hoodoo with humility and a willingness to learn from those who have practiced these traditions for generations. This may involve seeking out experienced practitioners and learning from them or engaging in serious research to better understand the cultural traditions that underpin these practices.

A Warning

It is important to approach the practice of Voodoo and Hoodoo with great respect and caution. These sacred traditions have been passed down through generations, and it is essential to understand their significance and power before attempting to engage in them. One of the most significant dangers of approaching Voodoo or Hoodoo without proper knowledge or guidance is the risk of invoking spirits inappropriately or disrespectfully. These spirits are not to be taken lightly or used for personal gain, and invoking them without proper preparation and intention can have serious consequences. It is common for those who attempt to practice Voodoo or Hoodoo without the proper knowledge to experience negative - or even dangerous - outcomes.

In many spiritual traditions, the act of invoking spirits is considered to be a powerful and potentially dangerous practice. In Voodoo and Hoodoo, this is no exception. In fact, it is of the utmost importance that anyone seeking to work with spirits in these traditions approaches the practice with respect, caution, and proper guidance. One of the primary risks of invoking spirits without proper initiation or guidance is the potential for harm to oneself or others. Spirits can be powerful entities with their own agendas, and they may not always be benevolent or helpful. If someone attempts to work with a spirit without proper knowledge or guidance, they may inadvertently invite in an evil entity or unintentionally offend one of the spirits, resulting in negative consequences such as illness, bad luck, or even physical harm.

Another risk of working with spirits without proper initiation or guidance is the potential for the practitioner to become unbalanced or unstable. In Voodoo and Hoodoo, there is a strong emphasis on spiritual and emotional balance, and this can be difficult to achieve without proper guidance. Attempting to work with spirits on one's own can result in a practitioner becoming too focused on the spiritual realm to the detriment of their physical and emotional well-being. Additionally, when someone works with spirits without proper initiation or guidance, they risk offending the spirits or the community of practitioners. Voodoo and Hoodoo are not casual spiritual practices. They are deeply rooted in specific cultural and historical contexts and are taken very seriously by those who practice them. Engaging in the practice without proper respect or reverence can be seen as disrespectful or appropriating; this could result in negative consequences both in the spiritual realm and in the wider community.

There have been many instances throughout history of individuals attempting to invoke spirits without proper guidance or initiation, with disastrous results. In some cases, malevolent entities have possessed practitioners, resulting in physical harm or death. In others, individuals have unintentionally offended powerful spirits, resulting in long-term misfortune or illness. In some cases, individuals who have attempted to practice Voodoo or Hoodoo without proper respect have been met with backlash from the wider community of practitioners, resulting in being ostracized or even being subject to violence.

That is why it is strongly advised against invoking any spirits or attempting spells and rituals from what you have heard. Instead, seeking guidance from an experienced practitioner or conducting serious research before practicing these traditions independently is recommended. An experienced practitioner can provide valuable guidance on approaching these practices respectfully. They can also guide you in finding a proper teacher or mentor who can provide further guidance on safely engaging in these traditions. Additionally, reading books or attending classes and workshops can provide a foundation of knowledge and understanding before attempting to practice.

Understanding that these are not mere parlor tricks or entertainment is essential. Voodoo and Hoodoo are serious spiritual practices with a rich cultural history and deep roots in African spirituality. They are not to be taken lightly or treated as a form of entertainment. The best way to approach these practices is with humility and a willingness to learn. It is essential to understand Voodoo and Hoodoo's cultural context and approach them with an open mind and deep respect for the traditions and spirits involved. It is also important to note that formal initiation is recommended in many Voodoo and Hoodoo traditions. Initiation involves a process of spiritual development, where you are taught the proper way to approach the spirits and how to use them in a respectful and responsible way. This is not a process to be taken lightly, as it involves a commitment to the tradition and to the spirits themselves.

Chapter Two: Bondye and the World

The concept of a supreme being is central to many religious and spiritual traditions, and Haitian Vodou, New Orleans Voodoo, and Hoodoo are no exception. In these practices, the Supreme Being is known as Bondye, a deity who is both mysterious and powerful and who is the creator of the universe and all life within it.

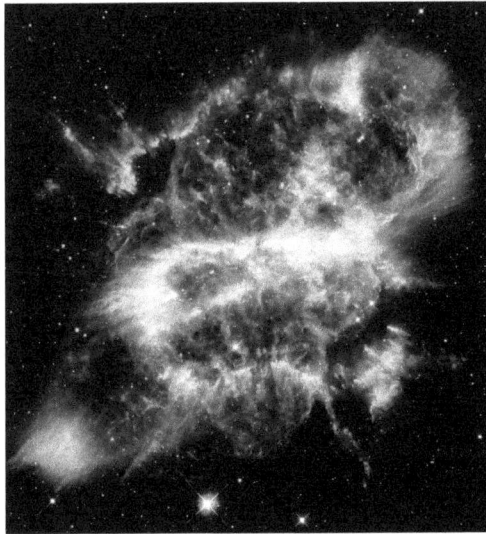

Bondye is the supreme being that created the universe.

On Bondye

Bondye is often described as being beyond human comprehension, existing in a realm beyond our understanding. His name is derived from the French phrase "Bon Dieu," which means "good God." This name is significant because it emphasizes Bondye's benevolent nature and distinguishes him from other spirits who may be more mischievous or malevolent in nature. Bondye represents a key element of Haitian Vodou, New Orleans Voodoo, and Hoodoo and serves as a powerful reminder of the mysteries and wonders of the natural world and our place within it. Bondye is often associated with white, representing purity and transcendence. Some practitioners believe that he is the same as the Christian God, while others see him as a distinct deity with his own characteristics and qualities.

According to Haitian Vodou, Bondye was the creator of the universe and all life within it. He is responsible for the cycles of life and death and is said to be present in every aspect of the natural world. The Loa, or spirits, are said to be intermediaries between Bondye and the physical world, allowing humans to communicate with the divine. Unlike the Loa, who are believed to be spirits of deceased ancestors and other beings, Bondye is seen as a purely divine and unchanging force. He is often associated with creation, order, and stability, while the Loa are associated with change, chaos, and transformation. New Orleans Voodoo and Hoodoo also recognize Bondye as the Supreme Being, but their beliefs and practices may differ in some ways from those of Haitian Vodou. For example, in Hoodoo, Bondye is often seen as less central to the practice than in Haitian Vodou, with greater emphasis placed on the use of herbs, roots, and other natural materials to work magic and influence the world you live in.

Despite these differences, the concept of Bondye as the Supreme Being remains a central part of all three traditions. Bondye is seen as a powerful and benevolent deity who holds the key to the mysteries of the universe and the cycles of life and death which govern this world. In many ways, he can be seen as a symbol of hope and transcendence, offering practitioners of Haitian Vodou, New Orleans Voodoo, and Hoodoo a way to connect with something greater than themselves and find meaning and purpose in a world that often seems chaotic and unpredictable.

At the same time, however, it is important to recognize the limitations of our understanding of Bondye and the spiritual realms which he inhabits. While the Loa may provide a means of communication between humanity and the divine, they are not infallible, and it is always important to approach spiritual practices with respect and caution, seeking guidance from experienced practitioners and doing your own research to deepen your understanding of these complex and powerful traditions.

How Bondye Made the World

The creation of the world is a central theme in the beliefs of many spiritual practices, and Haitian Vodou, New Orleans Voodoo, and Hoodoo are no exception. At the center of these practices is the belief in a supreme being, Bondye, who is credited with creating the world and all that is in it. In Haitian Vodou, Bondye is believed to have created the world through a process involving separating the earth from the sky and creating the first humans from clay. According to Haitian Vodou, the world was created in seven days, with each day representing a different aspect of creation. The first day was dedicated to the creation of the heavens, followed by the creation of the earth, the sea, the sun, the moon, animals, and finally, humans. This process of creation is seen as a reflection of Bondye's power and creativity, as well as symbolizing his ongoing relationship with the world and its inhabitants.

The creation story is slightly different in New Orleans Voodoo, but the basic themes remain the same. According to New Orleans Voodoo, Bondye created the world through a process of division, creating the physical world from a single source of energy. This process of division is seen as a reflection of Bondye's power and creativity and a symbol of his ongoing relationship with the world and its inhabitants.

Hoodoo, on the other hand, does not have a specific creation story. Rather, Hoodoo practitioners believe that the world was created by a combination of natural forces and spiritual energies, with Bondye as the ultimate source of these energies. This belief in a combination of natural and spiritual energies reflects Hoodoo's roots in African traditional religions, which often view the natural and spiritual worlds as interconnected and interdependent.

Despite the differences in their creation stories, all three practices emphasize the central role of Bondye in the creation of the world and the ongoing relationship between the divine and the physical world. This relationship is seen as an essential part of spiritual life, with practitioners often seeking to deepen their connection to Bondye through prayer, meditation, and ritual practice. It is worth noting that the creation stories of these practices are not meant to be taken literally but rather as symbolic representations of the relationship between the divine and the physical world. As with many other spiritual practices, the focus of belief is not on the details of the creation story itself but on the deeper meaning and symbolism behind it.

Haitian Vodou and Bondye

As the Supreme Being, Bondye plays a critical role in Haitian Vodou. Unlike the Lwa (or Loa), who are considered to be more accessible and can be invoked through ritual and prayer, Bondye is often seen as too distant to be directly contacted by human beings. He is a remote and powerful figure and is not typically worshiped in the same way as the Lwa. Instead, Haitian Vodou practitioners view Bondye as a distant observer of the world whose power is felt through his creations, including the Lwa and the natural world.

In Haitian Vodou, the relationship between humans and the divine is mediated through the Lwa, who are seen as the most active force in the universe. While the Lwa can be called upon for specific purposes such as healing, protection, or prosperity, Bondye is seen as the source of all these powers. Because of this, his influence is felt through the Lwa and their actions in the world.

The importance of Bondye in Haitian Vodou is also reflected in the religion's practices and rituals. Bondye is often invoked at the beginning and end of Vodou ceremonies, and his name is often used in blessings and prayers. However, because he is seen as too remote to be directly contacted, he is not typically the focus of Vodou worship. Instead, the Lwa are the main focus of most ceremonies, and it is through their presence that the power of Bondye is felt. One of the most important aspects of Bondye's role in Haitian Vodou is the belief that he is the source of all life and the universe. This story is often retold in Haitian Vodou ceremonies and is central to the religion's beliefs. It emphasizes the interconnectedness of all things and the idea that everything in the world is connected to Bondye, the ultimate source of power and creation.

New Orleans Voodoo and Bondye

In New Orleans Voodoo, Bondye is also recognized as the Supreme Being, but his role is slightly different from how he is seen in Haitian Vodou. The influence of Catholicism and the cultural context of New Orleans has contributed to the development of a unique form of Vodou emphasizing the intercession of saints and spirits in addition to how practitioners see Bondye. In New Orleans Voodoo, Bondye is often referred to as "Gran Met" or "Great Master" and is seen as the creator of the universe and all living things. Like Haitian Vodou, there is a belief in a dualistic cosmology, with the material and spiritual worlds existing simultaneously but separately. Bondye is seen as the source of all creation and is often depicted as a distant and powerful force. His communication with him is mediated through intermediaries such as spirits and saints.

However, unlike in Haitian Vodou, the spirits or "Lwa" in New Orleans Vodou are often viewed as having more direct influence and power over everyday life. This is due in part to the cultural influence of Louisiana, which has a history of folk practices and syncretism between Catholicism and African spiritual traditions. In New Orleans Voodoo, the spirits are seen as having the ability to intervene in human affairs and provide assistance or protection, and they are often the focus of veneration and ritual practices. Incorporating Catholicism, New Orleans Voodoo also recognizes the importance of saints in the spiritual realm, and many practitioners will invoke Catholic saints alongside the spirits of Vodou. This syncretic approach is also reflected in the use of Catholic iconography in Vodou rituals and the inclusion of elements such as candles and incense in Vodou practices.

Hoodoo and Bondye

In the tradition of Hoodoo, the role of Bondye is somewhat different from the way he is viewed in Haitian and New Orleans Voodoo. Bondye is seen as the ultimate creator and source of all spiritual power, but he is not typically worshiped or invoked directly in Hoodoo practices. Instead, practitioners of Hoodoo often focus on working with individual spirits and spiritual forces to achieve their desired outcomes.

Bondye still plays an important role in Hoodoo as the ultimate source of all spiritual power. Many Hoodoo practitioners believe that all spirits and spiritual forces are ultimately under Bondye's control and can be called upon through the power of his name. In some Hoodoo traditions, the name "Bon Dieu" (meaning "good God" in French, a legacy of Hoodoo's Creole roots) is used as a general term for any divine or spiritual force that can be called upon for assistance.

One of the key differences between Hoodoo and the Vodou traditions is that Hoodoo does not typically involve formal initiation or membership in a specific religious community. Instead, Hoodoo is often passed down through families or acquired through personal study and practice. As a result, depending on their personal beliefs and experiences, individual practitioners may have different views on the role of Bondye and other spiritual forces in their practice. Despite these differences, however, many Hoodoo practitioners still deeply respect Bondye as the ultimate source of all spiritual power. They may use his name in prayers or invocations or may seek to align themselves with his divine will in their magical work. Ultimately, the role of Bondye in Hoodoo is a complex and multifaceted one, reflecting the diverse spiritual beliefs and practices of this unique African American folk tradition.

On the Loa

First, it is essential to understand that the Loa (or Lwa) are not gods in the traditional sense. They are not omnipotent, omnipresent, or omniscient. Instead, they are beings with unique personalities and specific areas of expertise. Each Loa has its own distinct history, mythology, and abilities. Some are associated with particular places, while others are connected to specific aspects of life, such as love, health, or wealth. The Loa are believed to be powerful spiritual entities that can provide guidance, protection, and blessings to those who worship them.

The relationship between Bondye and the Loa is a complex one. Bondye is considered the Supreme Being, the creator of the universe, and the source of all life. The Loa, on the other hand, are seen as intermediaries, bridging the gap between the physical and the spiritual world. They are believed to be the spirits of those who have passed on and are now part of the spiritual realm. Some believe that the Loa were originally humans who achieved a higher spiritual state after death and were elevated to a position of divine influence. Others believe that the Loa are independent spirits that have always existed and were simply acknowledged and incorporated into Vodou practices over time. In either case, it is believed that Bondye gave the Loa their power and authority to interact with humans and affect the physical world. The exact details of how the Loa were created and by whom vary among different Vodou traditions and interpretations.

The Loa work with Bondye to provide spiritual guidance and blessings to practitioners. In Haitian Vodou and New Orleans Voodoo, the Loa are summoned through rituals and ceremonies that involve music, dance, and offerings. Practitioners often make offerings to the Loa, such as food, alcohol, or flowers, to establish a relationship and gain their favor. The Loa are believed to have a particular fondness for certain types of offerings and may be more likely to provide blessings when they are presented with their preferred gifts.

In Hoodoo, the relationship between the Loa and practitioners is less formal. While the Loa are still considered powerful spirits, Hoodoo practitioners may not perform formal ceremonies or make offerings to them. Instead, the Loa may be called upon in spells or rituals to provide guidance or protection. Hoodoo practitioners may also work with other spirits, such as ancestors or guardian angels, in addition to the Loa.

It's important to note that the Loa are not all-powerful. They cannot grant every request, and they may not always answer prayers in the way that practitioners expect. While the Loa are believed to have the power to influence the physical world, they are also subject to the laws of nature and the will of Bondye. Some practitioners may mistakenly assume that the Loa are omnipotent, leading to disappointment or disillusionment when their prayers are not answered as expected.

Additionally, the Loa are often misunderstood as gods or demons by those who are unfamiliar with Haitian Vodou, New Orleans Voodoo, and Hoodoo. This misconception may be partly due to the Loas' powerful abilities and unique personalities. Some Loa are associated with darker aspects of life, such as death or disease, which may contribute to the idea that they are malevolent beings. However, this is a misunderstanding of their role in these practices. The Loa are not worshiped in the same way as gods or demons and are not seen as being fundamentally different from human beings. Instead, they are considered to be part of the spiritual realm, just like ancestors and guardian angels.

Please don't attempt to go directly to Bondye. Bondye is considered too powerful and too remote for most humans to communicate effectively, making direct communication difficult, if not impossible. Don't take this to mean that the good God doesn't care about you and your affairs. He does, and that's why he has sent intermediaries so you can communicate with each other through them. Also, trying to invoke him would be disrespectful to all Vodou practices. If you consider that your problem is so urgent that only Bondye can help, it is recommended that you seek the guidance of an experienced practitioner of Vodou, who can help you to communicate with the divine in a safe and effective way. This may involve ritual purification, offerings to the Loa, and the guidance of an intermediary who is experienced in communicating with the divine.

Chapter Three: Voodoo Allies: The Lwa and the Ancestors

The Lwa, or Loa, are spirits who play a significant role in the African diasporic religion of Voodoo. In Haitian Voodoo, the Lwa are organized into seven "nanchons" or "nations," each with its own characteristics, symbols, and rituals. Understanding the nature of each nanchon is important for Voodoo practitioners, as it guides the selection of appropriate offerings, songs, and dances to invoke the Lwa. In New Orleans Voodoo, there are only three nanchons: The Rada, Petro, and Gede nanchons. As for Hoodoo, there isn't a lot of emphasis placed on the classifications of these spirits.

The Lwa or Loa are spirits that play an important role in Voodoo.

The Haitian Vodou Nanchons

The Rada Lwa: The first nanchon is Rada, also known as Radha. The Rada Lwa are considered to be the oldest of the seven nations of Lwa and are associated with the spirits of the Fon people of Dahomey. Their traditions emphasize harmony, peace, and healing. The Rada Lwa are often called upon to resolve conflicts, heal illnesses, and bring prosperity to their followers. The symbols associated with the Rada Lwa are generally round and symmetrical, and their veves often include circles and intersecting lines. The Rada Lwa are often invoked through drumming and dancing, as well as through the use of specific herbal remedies and spiritual baths. Followers of the Rada tradition may also offer gifts and sacrifices to the Lwa, such as food, drink, and animal sacrifices.

The Petro Lwa: The second nanchon is Petro, also known as Pethro or Petwo. These fierce and fiery entities have a reputation for being some of the most dangerous and unpredictable in the Vodou religion. The Petro Lwa are associated with the spirits of the Haitian Revolution, and their traditions emphasize power, resistance, and revolution. These spirits are often called upon to help their followers fight against oppression and injustice, and they are known for their ability to unleash powerful forces of destruction against their enemies. The symbols associated with the Petro Lwa are generally jagged and asymmetrical, and their veves often include zig-zags and sharp angles.

The spirits in this nation are also known for their association with fire and blood. These powerful forces are believed to be the key to unlocking the full potential of the Petro Lwa, and many of their rituals involve the use of fire and blood to activate their powers. However, the power of the Petro Lwa is not without its risks. These spirits are known for their volatile and unpredictable nature, and they are not to be trifled with. Those seeking to work with the Petro Lwa must approach with caution and respect and be prepared to deal with the consequences of their actions.

Furthermore, the Petro Lwa are often misunderstood and maligned by those outside of the Vodou community. They are sometimes associated with dark magic and evil forces, and their followers are often demonized and persecuted. This is a tragic misunderstanding of the true nature of the Petro Lwa, and it highlights the importance of education and understanding when it comes to the Vodou religion.

The Nago Lwa: The Nago nation of Lwa is a group of spirits deeply rooted in the African Yoruba religion. They are known for their fierce and warrior-like qualities. They are often called upon to help with matters related to protection, justice, and strength. It is said that the Nago Lwa possess a deep and intimate knowledge of the secrets of the universe and that they hold the keys to unlocking the mysteries of life and death. The veves associated with this nanchon of Lwa are intricate and complex, often featuring patterns of interlocking lines and geometric shapes. These symbols are thought to represent the complex and intertwined nature of the universe and the interconnectedness of all living things.

In the Vodou tradition, the Nago Lwa are associated with the color red, which is said to represent their fiery and passionate nature. They are often depicted with weapons or symbols of war, such as spears or swords, and are known for their fierce and uncompromising nature. However, despite their warrior-like qualities, these Lwa are also deeply compassionate and caring. Known for their ability to heal, both physically and spiritually, they are often called upon to help those who are suffering from a specific illness or emotional distress. The Lwa are also associated with the element of fire, which is seen as a purifying and transformative force. They are said to have the power to burn away negative energies and help those who seek guidance to rise from the ashes of their past and be reborn anew.

To approach the Nago Lwa is to enter into a world of mystery and power, where the boundaries between the physical and spiritual realms blur and dissolve. Those who seek their guidance must do so with respect and reverence, for the Nago Lwa are not to be trifled with. Despite their fearsome reputation, the Nago Lwa are deeply committed to helping those who seek their guidance. They are known for their fierce loyalty and unwavering dedication to their followers and will go to great lengths to ensure that those seeking their aid are protected and supported.

The Kongo Lwa: The Kongo nanchon of Lwa is a powerful force in the world of Voodoo. Their traditions are deeply rooted in the culture and history of the people of the Kongo taken to Haiti as slaves. The Kongo Lwa are associated with the spirits of the Kongo people, and their traditions emphasize strength, courage, and resilience. They are often called upon to help their followers overcome obstacles and find success in difficult circumstances.

The Kongo Lwa are organized into four families or groups: Lemba, Simbi, Mayisi, and Ti-Jean Petro. Each family has its own set of spirits and traditions, but they are all united by a deep sense of pride and a fierce devotion to their followers. The Lemba family is perhaps the most well-known of the Kongo nanchon. They are associated with the spirits of the royal court of the Kongo kingdom, and their traditions emphasize justice, order, and stability. The Lemba Lwa are often called upon to help resolve disputes and bring peace to their followers. Their veves are often very detailed and intricate, featuring complex geometric patterns and interlocking shapes.

The Simbi family is associated with the spirits of the water, and their traditions emphasize healing and transformation. The Simbi Lwa are often called upon to help heal physical and emotional ailments and to bring about positive changes in their followers' lives. Their veves often feature images of snakes and other water creatures, as well as flowing lines and curves. The Mayisi family is associated with the spirits of the forest, and their traditions emphasize protection and strength. The Mayisi Lwa are often called upon to help their followers overcome obstacles and defend themselves against harm. Their veves often feature images of trees, animals, and other symbols of the forest.

Finally, the Ti-Jean Petro family is associated with the spirits of the Earth, and their traditions emphasize power and transformation. The Ti-Jean Petro Lwa are often called upon to help their followers achieve their goals and overcome their fears. Their veves are often very bold and dramatic, featuring powerful images of fire and earth.

The Djouba Lwa: The fifth nanchon is Djouba, which is associated with the spirits of the Mandinga people of West Africa. The Djouba Lwa are known for their energy and vitality, and they are often called upon to help with fertility, creativity, and inspiration. The Djouba Lwa are also associated with the sun's power and are sometimes invoked to bring light and warmth to their followers. The symbols associated with the Djouba Lwa often include circles, spirals, and sunbursts.

The Djouba nanchon of Lwa, a powerful and enigmatic force within the voodoo religion, embodies a complex web of influences and traditions that span both time and space.

But despite their elusive and often otherworldly nature, the Djouba remain an essential part of voodoo practice, revered for their ability to bring prosperity, good luck, and healing to those who call upon them.

One of the most powerful symbols associated with the Djouba nanchon is the crossroads, which represents the intersection of different worlds and the possibility of new beginnings. It is believed that the Djouba Lwa inhabit the crossroads, guiding and protecting those who seek their help.

But the Djouba are not simply passive guardians of the crossroads. They are also active agents of change and transformation, capable of bringing about profound shifts in the lives of their followers. Through their rituals and offerings, the Djouba can heal illness, bring good fortune, and even help to find love. Yet, despite their many gifts and powers, the Djouba nanchon remains a mystery to many outsiders, their true nature and significance known only to those who have earned their trust and respect. To the uninitiated, the Djouba may seem capricious and unpredictable, and their actions and desires difficult to understand.

However, for those who have experienced the transformative power of the Djouba, there is no doubt that these Lwa are a force to be reckoned with as agents of change and transformation who hold the key to unlocking new possibilities and potential. In many ways, the Djouba nanchon embodies the spirit of Voodoo itself, a complex and dynamic tradition that draws upon the wisdom and knowledge of many different cultures and traditions. Like the Lwa themselves, voodoo is a force that transcends boundaries, connecting people across time and space and helping them to navigate the challenges and opportunities of life.

The Ibo Lwa: The sixth nanchon is Ibo, which is associated with the spirits of the Igbo people of Nigeria. The Ibo Lwa are known for their ability to communicate with the spiritual realm, and they are often called upon to help with divination and prophecy. The Ibo Lwa are also associated with the power of the wind, and they are sometimes invoked to bring change and transformation.

The Ibo Lwa are known for their deep connection to nature, drawing inspiration from the earth, the sky, and the spirits that dwell within them. They are fierce protectors of their followers, shielding them from harm and guiding them toward the path of righteousness. Their veves are intricate and complex, depicting the intricate balance between the natural world and the spiritual realm. The Ibo Lwa are often called upon for matters related to justice and morality, and they hold a special place in the hearts of those who seek guidance in times of trouble.

But their power does not come without sacrifice. The Ibo people have faced countless hardships throughout their history, from the horrors of slavery to the brutal colonization of their land. And yet, through it all, they have persevered, holding onto their traditions and their connection to the spirits that guide them. The Ibo Lwa reflect this perseverance, embodying the strength and determination of their people. Their rituals are steeped in tradition, each one carefully crafted to honor the spirits and invoke their power. The rhythms of the drums and the sway of the dancers serve as a conduit, channeling the energy of the spirits and bringing it into the world.

The Ibo Lwa are also associated with the power of knowledge and education. They understand that true power comes not only from physical strength but from the strength of the mind and the wisdom of the soul. They are teachers and guides, imparting their knowledge to those who seek it and helping them to grow and evolve.

The Ghede Lwa: The Ghede nanchon of Lwa is a mysterious and powerful group of spirits known for their connection to death and the afterlife. They are both feared and revered, and their presence is felt throughout the Vodou religion. They are often called upon to help with matters related to death, and their traditions emphasize humor, sexuality, and fertility. In the world of Vodou, they are gatekeepers, holding the key to the mysteries of life and death.

There is a certain mystique surrounding the Ghede nanchon. They are considered outsiders, and their traditions are often misunderstood by those who have little knowledge of the religion. But for those who practice Vodou, the Ghede Lwa is essential to the spiritual landscape. They are a reminder of the fragility of life and the importance of honoring those who have passed on. This nanchon is made up of a diverse group of spirits, each with its own unique attributes and personalities. Some are known for their raucous behavior, while others are more serious and contemplative. But all of them share a deep connection to death and a powerful ability to help guide the souls of the departed.

The Ghede nanchon is also home to many important spirits, each with its own unique personality and role within the nanchon. But despite their differences, they all share a deep connection to the world of the dead and a powerful ability to help those who are struggling with issues related to death and the afterlife. This nanchon is often seen as a symbol of the circle of life; it is a reminder that death is not an end but rather a transition to a new phase of existence. The Ghede Lwa are seen as guides, helping ease the passage of the soul from the physical world to the world beyond.

They also remind one and all of the importance of living life to the fullest. They are known for their raucous celebrations and their love of dance, music, and sex. The Ghede Lwa are a reminder that life is short and that it should be lived with joy and passion. In many ways, they embody the contradictions that are at the heart of the Vodou religion. They are both serious and irreverent, powerful and playful, revered and feared.

On Veves

A "veve" is a symbolic design or drawing representing a specific Lwa or spirit. These intricate designs are created using a variety of materials, including cornmeal, flour, and ashes, and are typically drawn on the ground or on a piece of cloth or paper. The creation of a veve is an important part of invoking a particular Lwa and inviting their presence into a ceremony or ritual. The importance of veves lies in their ability to create a visual connection between the practitioner and the Lwa. Each veve is unique and has specific symbols and patterns corresponding to the attributes and qualities of a particular spirit. For example, the veve for the Lwa Legba (associated with communication and gatekeeping) often includes keys or a crossroads.

When a veve is created, it is accompanied by prayers, chants, and offerings to the Lwa, all of which serve to amplify the practitioner's intent and focus their energy on a specific outcome. Through this process, the veve becomes a powerful tool to invoke the spirit and open up a channel for communication and exchange. However, it is important to note that the use of veves is not a casual or frivolous practice. In recent years, there has been an increase in the mindless use of veves in popular culture, with people tattooing them on their bodies without a clear understanding of their significance or the traditions they are connected to. This trend has led to concerns about cultural appropriation and the commodification of Vodou practices.

Using veves requires respect and understanding of their cultural and spiritual significance. Practitioners must approach the creation and use of veves with clear intent and a deep reverence for the Lwa they represent. This means taking the time to learn about the specific meanings and associations of each veve and understanding the proper protocols for invoking and working with the associated spirit. If you don't use these symbols respectfully, the Lwa may choose to ignore you permanently, or the moodier spirits may punish you for insulting them with your careless use of their symbol. Please understand that veves are not simply decorative designs or symbols to be used for personal gain. They are powerful tools for spiritual transformation and must be used with the utmost care and respect. Veves should only be created and used by those who have undergone proper training and initiation in Vodou traditions and have a deep understanding of the spiritual dimensions of their work.

Your Ancestors

In the vast realm of Voodoo and Hoodoo practices, one cannot overstate the importance of ancestors. The revered ones who have passed before us carry with them the wisdom of the ages, the knowledge of the mysteries of the universe, and the accumulated experiences of their lives. They are the guardians of our lineages, the keepers of your heritage, and the spirits who can guide you toward your destiny. The ancestors are considered the first line of defense, the first point of contact, and the first bridge between the human and the spirit world. They serve as a conduit for the Lwa and are believed to be able to communicate with the ancestors. Thus, invoking the help of the ancestors is a crucial step in any Voodoo or Hoodoo practice.

These spirits are vital because they can offer guidance, protection, and healing. They can also provide spiritual nourishment, blessings, and abundance. They are believed to be able to intervene in the lives of their descendants, particularly in times of need, crisis, or danger. They can help practitioners overcome obstacles, break curses, and succeed in their endeavors.

Contacting Your Ancestors

To contact your ancestors, you must set up an ancestor altar, which can be a simple or elaborate arrangement of photographs, candles, flowers, and offerings. You can then light candles and incense, offer food, drink, or tobacco, and meditate or pray in front of the altar. The goal is to create a sacred space where the ancestors can feel welcomed and honored and where you can communicate with them.

As a beginner Voodooist, you should establish a connection with your ancestors before you attempt to contact the Lwa directly. This is because the ancestors are considered the gateway to the spirit world and can help you navigate the complexities of Voodoo and Hoodoo practices. By establishing a relationship with your ancestors, you can better understand your roots, your lineage, and your place in the world. Your ancestors can also be a source of inspiration, creativity, and intuition. They can guide you toward your purpose, calling, and destiny.

You can access the collective wisdom of your ancestors through your community, culture, and traditions. The ancestors can even help you develop your psychic abilities, divination skills, and other spiritual gifts. However, it is essential to approach the ancestors with respect, humility, and sincerity. They are not to be taken lightly, for they are powerful spirits who demand reverence and gratitude. The ancestors must be honored, fed, and regularly remembered, for they are the foundation of our lives and the guardians of our spirits.

Chapter Four: The Rada Lwa

This chapter teaches you about the cool and gentle Rada spirits. These spirits are beginner-friendly, more so than their fiery and unpredictable Petro counterparts.

Ezili Freda

Ezili Freda is a graceful and elegant Lwa, a divine spirit of love, beauty, femininity, and luxury. She is often depicted as a beautiful woman dressed in white, adorned with pearls, and holding a fan or a mirror. Her presence is calming and soothing, and her energy is nurturing and powerful. Her veve, a sacred symbol used to invoke her presence, is intricately designed with a central heart and feathers, flowers, and other symbols of beauty surrounding it. White and other pastel shades (like pink and blue) are often associated with her. She is also associated with the fragrance of jasmine and other sweet-scented flowers.

In Haitian Vodou, Ezili Freda is syncretized with the Catholic saint, Our Lady of Lourdes; she is often called upon for healing and comfort. She is associated with the concept of pure, unconditional love and is revered for her ability to bring harmony and balance to relationships. She is often paired with the powerful and virile Lwa, Damballa, and together they represent the divine union of male and female energy. She is also associated with other gentle and loving Lwa like Agwe, LaSiren, and Loco.

Ezili Freda is syncretized with Our Lady of Lourdes.
Wayne S. Grazio, CC BY-NC-ND 2.0 DEED < https://creativecommons.org/licenses/by-nc-nd/2.0/>https://www.flickr.com/photos/fotograzio/17993185248

Lore surrounding Ezili Freda often depicts her as a beautiful and vain woman who enjoys luxury and the finer things in life. She is known for her love of pearls and other precious jewels, and offerings of these items are often made to her. She is also known for her gentle nature and ability to soothe troubled hearts and bring peace to difficult situations. To honor Ezili Freda, practitioners often offer her gifts of champagne, white flowers, and sweets. It is said that if she accepts an offering, she will leave a sign such as the presence of a butterfly, a scent of perfume, or a feeling of calm and love.

Ezili Freda is honored during Carnival season with the Krewe of Muses parade, which features her as their patron Lwa. Mardi Gras Indians also honor her with their elaborate beadwork and feathered costumes. Ezili Freda is a beloved and powerful Lwa who offers guidance, love, and protection to those seeking her out. Her energy is a reminder of the power of love and the beauty of the divine feminine.

There are many real-life stories of individuals who have established a deep and meaningful connection with Ezili Freda. One such story is that of Marie, a young woman from New Orleans. Marie had always been drawn to the spiritual traditions of her ancestors, but it wasn't until she discovered the practice of Vodou that she truly found a sense of belonging. From the moment she first saw Ezili Freda's veve, Marie knew that she had found her spiritual home.

Over time, Marie began to incorporate the veneration of Ezili Freda into her daily practice. She would light candles and offer flowers and other gifts to the spirit, always with a sense of deep reverence and respect.

One day, Marie received a powerful sign that her offerings had been accepted by Ezili Freda. She was walking down the street when she saw a butterfly, its wings the same shade of pink as the flowers she had offered to the spirit earlier that day. As she watched, the butterfly landed on her shoulder and remained there for several minutes before flying away. From that moment on, Marie knew she had a special connection with Ezili Freda. She continued to offer gifts and revere the spirit. In return, she felt a sense of love and protection she had never experienced.

Agwe

Agwe, the ruler of the seas and oceans, is a majestic and powerful Lwa revered by many in the Voodoo and Hoodoo traditions. He is often depicted as a handsome and muscular man with green scales and a mermaid tail, reflecting his association with water. His veve is an intricate symbol of a ship with sails, surrounded by waves and fish, representing his dominion over the seas. Other symbols associated with him include sea shells, coral, and fish hooks.

Agwe is the ruler of the seas.

In the syncretic tradition of Haitian Vodou, Agwe is often associated with the Catholic saint, St. Ulrich, who is also associated with the sea. This syncretism highlights the complex interweaving of African and European traditions that characterize Voodoo and Hoodoo traditions. Agwe's correspondences include the colors blue and green and plants and herbs associated with the ocean, such as seaweed and sea salt. He is also associated with rum, a popular offering to him. He shares close ties with La Sirène and Simbi Andezo.

Agwe is a fierce and protective spirit, willing to do whatever it takes to protect his devotees. He is known to be generous and kind – but also powerful and dangerous when angered. Offerings to Agwe often take the form of food, drink, and other gifts left at the shore or tossed into the sea. Signs that he has received and accepted one's offerings may include calm waters, a successful fishing trip, or other signs of good fortune on the water. Agwe is often celebrated and honored in various ways, including through rituals and offerings at the shore or other bodies of water. The Krewe of Proteus, a Mardi Gras organization founded in 1882, has chosen Agwe as its official patron, reflecting the enduring popularity of this powerful and beloved Lwa in the city's cultural traditions.

Legba

Legba, the guardian of the crossroads, is one of the most important and beloved Lwa in the Voodoo pantheon. He is a wise and mischievous old man, often depicted with a staff and a straw hat, and is known to speak in riddles and cryptic messages. His veve is a simple yet powerful symbol, consisting of a crossroads with a circle at the center. His colors are red and black, and his correspondences include tobacco, rum, and palm oil. He is associated with the herb rue and the plant hibiscus and is syncretized with Saint Peter in the Catholic tradition.

A statue of Legba, the gatekeeper between the human and spirit worlds.
Jeremy Burgin, CC BY-SA 2.0 <https://creativecommons.org/licenses/by-sa/2.0>, via Wikimedia Commons https://commons.wikimedia.org/wiki/File:Statue-of-Legba-by-Jeremy-Burgin.jpg

Legba is closely linked with other Lwa, such as Papa Ghede and Baron Samedi, and is said to be the gatekeeper between the human and spirit worlds. He is also known for removing obstacles and providing opportunities, making him a popular choice for those seeking guidance and luck. Often portrayed as a trickster, he uses wit and humor to teach important lessons and keep people on their toes. He is a protector of children and the elderly and revered for his wisdom and ability to see everything.

To honor Legba, offerings of rum, tobacco, and food are often given at crossroads, and his veve is drawn in powdered cornmeal or flour. Signs that he has accepted an offering may include a sudden gust of wind, the sound of footsteps, or the appearance of a stray dog. Legba is celebrated during the annual Voodoo Fest, as well as during Mardi Gras and other festivities. His presence can be felt throughout the city in the music, the food, and the spirit of its people. Legba is a wise and trusted friend for those seeking his guidance and protection.

Loco

Loco is a figure of tremendous strength and vitality, able to move mountains and stir up mighty storms. Often depicted as a tall and muscular man with a fierce and commanding presence, his face is adorned with intricate tribal markings, and his eyes shine with a fierce and unyielding light. He holds a staff of pure gold in his hands, symbolizing his strength and dominion over the elements. One of the most striking symbols associated with Loco is his veve, a powerful and intricate design that represents his presence and power. The veve of Loco features a series of concentric circles, each containing a different symbol or image that represents some aspect of his essence.

In the syncretic traditions of New Orleans, Loco is often associated with the Catholic Saint Anthony of Padua. This connection reflects Loco's role as a guide and protector of the downtrodden and marginalized and his reputation as a miraculous healer and provider of sustenance. In terms of correspondence, Loco is often associated with the color green and various herbs and plants such as mint, basil, and vervain. These correspondences reflect his connection to the natural world and his ability to channel its energies to achieve his goals.

The veve of Loco.

Sam Fentress, CC BY-SA 2.0 <https://creativecommons.org/licenses/by-sa/2.0>, via Wikimedia Commons https://commons.wikimedia.org/wiki/File:VoodooValris.jpg

In terms of his relations with other Loa, Loco is often depicted as a powerful ally of Damballa, the serpent spirit of creation, as well as with other figures associated with the natural world, such as Oya and Oshun. He is also said to be fiercely protective of his followers and is not afraid to act against those who seek to harm them. Loco is often depicted as a spirit of great power and mystery, capable of performing miraculous feats and providing guidance and support to those in need. He is also said to possess a fiercely independent streak and is not afraid to challenge authority or convention in pursuit of his goals. Preferred offerings to Loco may include items such as cigars, rum, and other potent spirits, as well as various food items such as chicken, fish, and rice. Signs that Loco has received and accepted one's offerings may include sudden shifts in the weather or the appearance of various animals such as snakes, lizards, or other creatures associated with the natural world.

This Loa is celebrated and honored during various festivals and observances throughout the year, particularly during the annual Mardi Gras celebrations. During these events, offerings are made to Loco to seek his protection and guidance, and various rituals and ceremonies are performed to honor his power and influence.

Damballa

Damballa, the serpent spirit, is a powerful Loa of Haitian Vodou. He is often depicted as a giant white serpent coiled around a staff or as a rainbow. Damballa is associated with creation, wisdom, and the primal forces of the universe. His symbol, the veve, is a stylized representation of a serpent. In Haitian Vodou, this Loa is often syncretized with Saint Patrick, the patron saint of Ireland. His correspondences include the color white, the herb basil, and the plant hibiscus. Damballa is closely associated with his consort, Ayida-Weddo, the rainbow serpent. Together, they represent the universe's balance of masculine and feminine energies. Damballa is also associated with other powerful Loa, such as Papa Legba and Baron Samedi.

Damballa, the serpent spirit.
https://commons.wikimedia.org/wiki/File:Damballah_La_Flambeau.jpg

---

Lore connected to Damballa depicts him as a wise, benevolent spirit willing to guide and protect his devotees. He is known to be a powerful healer and is often called upon to cure illness or to provide guidance in matters of wisdom and knowledge. Devotees often offer him eggs, milk, and white rum as offerings, which are placed at his altar. Signs that he has received and accepted an offering include the appearance of snakes in the area or the sound of hissing. Damballa is celebrated and honored during various Voodoo ceremonies throughout the year, including the Feast of St. John and the Festival of the Dead. During these celebrations, offerings are given, and prayers are made to Damballa, and his powerful presence is felt by those who attend.

Ayizan

Ayizan is a powerful Loa in the Vodou tradition, known for her ability to connect individuals with the divine and spiritual world. She is often depicted as an elderly woman dressed in white or blue and adorned with cowrie shells and a broom, which symbolize her role as the temple keeper. Her veve, or sacred symbol, is a cross with a horizontal line at the top, and it is often drawn in white or blue on the ground during Vodou ceremonies. Other symbols associated with Ayizan include the broom, cowrie shells, and the acacia tree.

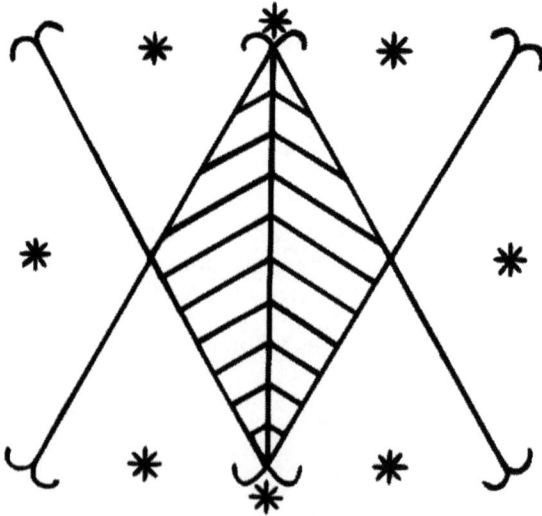

The veve for Ayizan.
https://commons.wikimedia.org/wiki/File:VeveAyizan.svg

Ayizan is sometimes syncretized with the Catholic saint, Our Lady of Mount Carmel, who is also associated with brooms and spiritual cleansing. Her correspondences include the colors white and blue, as well as herbs like rosemary, basil, and lavender. In Vodou, she is often called upon to open the door between the physical and spiritual worlds, allowing for communication with the divine. She is also associated with fertility, healing, and protection and is said to possess a kind and nurturing personality.

According to lore, Ayizan was the first Mambo, or priestess, in the Vodou tradition. She taught others how to communicate with the Loa and was instrumental in spreading the practice throughout Haiti and beyond. Offerings to her often include items such as white candles, brooms, and cowrie shells, as well as food and drink like cornmeal, water, and rum. Signs that Ayizan has received and accepted an offering may include the sound of a broom sweeping the floor or a feeling of spiritual clarity and connection. Ayizan is often celebrated and honored as part of the Vodou tradition, particularly during the annual Voodoo Fest in October. She is also revered by many in the Haitian community, who continue to practice the ancient traditions she helped establish so long ago.

Chapter Five: The Gede Lwa

In this chapter, you'll learn about the most popular Gede Lwa, starting with Baron Samedi.

Baron Samedi

Baron Samedi, the Lord of the Dead, is a complex and multifaceted Loa in the Haitian Vodou tradition. His image is that of a tall, thin man with sunken eyes and a skull-like face. He wears a top hat and a long black coat and is often seen carrying a cane. Despite his fearsome appearance, he is known to be a jovial and charming spirit with a deep sense of humor and a love of life. The veve of Baron Samedi is a simple design consisting of a cross with two small vertical lines on either side. He is also associated with the image of a skull and crossbones, representing his role as the ruler of the dead. In Haitian Vodou, Baron Samedi is syncretized with Saint Martin de Porres, a Peruvian lay brother known for his healing powers and devotion to the poor and the sick.

Baron Samedi, the Loa of death.
Nicolas Munoz, CC BY-NC-SA 2.0 DEED < https://creativecommons.org/licenses/by-nc-sa/2.0/ > https://www.flickr.com/photos/nicolasmunoz/5817315380

Baron Samedi is closely associated with death but also with fertility and rebirth. His colors are black and purple, and his correspondences include tobacco, rum, and coffee. He is often invoked to help with matters related to love and fertility, as well as for protection and healing. In Haitian Vodou, Baron Samedi is considered the leader of the Gede, a group of Loa associated with death and the afterlife. He is married to the powerful Loa Maman Brigitte and is often seen in the company of other Gede spirits, such as Baron La Croix and Baron Kriminel.

Despite his macabre image, Baron Samedi is a beloved and respected figure in Haitian Vodou, known for his wisdom, wit, and ability to help those in need. Devotees of Baron Samedi offer him offerings of tobacco, rum, and other items associated with death and the afterlife. Signs that he has accepted an offering may include the appearance of a black butterfly or the scent of tobacco smoke. Baron Samedi is celebrated as part of the annual Voodoo Festival, which takes place each year in October. Devotees of Vodou honor him by leaving offerings at his altar, dancing and singing in his honor, and participating in rituals and ceremonies designed to honor his power and influence.

Maman Brigitte

Maman Brigitte is a powerful Lwa in the Vodou pantheon with a voice like molasses and a presence like thunder. She is often depicted as a tall, striking woman with fiery red hair and piercing green eyes. She wears a long, flowing dress and carries a machete or a bottle of rum. Her veve is a cross with a circle in the center, and her associated symbols include black roosters, red and black candles, and hot peppers.

In Haitian Vodou, Maman Brigitte is syncretized with the Catholic saint Brigid and is often called upon for protection, justice, and healing. She is associated with death, the afterlife, healing, and transformation. Her colors are black and purple, and her corresponding herbs include basil, bay leaf, and rosemary.

Maman Brigitte is said to have a close relationship with Baron Samedi, the Lwa of death, and is often seen as his wife or sister. She is also associated with the Ghede, a group of Lwa who are the spirits of the dead. She is known for her fierce, protective nature and ability to help those in trouble or facing difficult situations. She is also said to have a mischievous side and enjoys playing pranks on those who do not show her proper respect. Maman Brigitte is a fierce warrior and protector of women. She is also renowned for her love of rum and tobacco, and offerings of these items are said to please her.

Other offerings that are said to please her include black roosters, hot peppers, and red and black candles. Maman Brigitte is celebrated in Haitian Vodou during the Festival of the Dead, which takes place in November. She is honored during the Vodou-inspired Mardi Gras celebrations and the Day of the Dead festivities. She is often invoked for protection and healing, as well as for guidance and strength during times of difficulty. Her presence is felt in the fiery energy of New Orleans, and she is often called upon for her powerful and protective energy.

Baron La Croix

Baron La Croix is one of the lesser-known Loa in the Vodou pantheon, but he is no less powerful or revered. He is often depicted as a man with a fierce countenance dressed in black and white and carrying a walking stick. His veve is a complex pattern of intersecting lines and shapes, often incorporating the colors black, white, and red. This Baron is not syncretized with any Catholic saint, but he does have correspondences to various colors, herbs, and plants. He is associated with black, which represents death and the underworld. Some of the herbs and plants associated with him include horehound, rue, and tobacco.

Baron La Croix has a unique relationship with the other Loa. He is often considered a solitary figure, rarely interacting with other spirits. However, he is sometimes invoked with other Loa, especially those associated with death and the underworld, such as Baron Samedi and Maman Brigitte. There is not much lore surrounding Baron La Croix, but those who have worked with him describe him as a powerful and mysterious force. He is said to be a master of transformation and can help those who seek to change their lives in significant ways.

Preferred offerings for Baron La Croix include rum, cigars, and black candles. Signs that he has received and accepted an offering may include mysterious coincidences, vivid dreams, or a sense of closure or completion. He is not widely celebrated or honored, but some practitioners of Vodou may include him in their personal spiritual practices. He is considered a potent and enigmatic force to be approached with caution and respect.

Baron Cimetière

In Haitian Vodou, Baron Cimetière is often depicted as a skeletal figure wearing a top hat and carrying a cane or a shovel. He is associated with death, cemeteries, and the spirits of the dead. He is also considered to be the guardian of the cemetery and the gatekeeper between the living and the dead. His veve depicts a skull with crossed bones; his colors are black and purple. His offerings include rum, cigars, and black coffee, and his sacred herbs include rue, basil, and lavender. If he seems similar to Baron Samedi, that's because he is another aspect of that Gede Lwa.

Baron Cimetière has strong relationships with other spirits of death and the dead, including Papa Ghede and Maman Brigitte. He is also associated with the Catholic saint, Saint Expeditus, and syncretized with him in some traditions. Regarding lore, the Baron is said to be feared and respected by those working with him. He is known for his blunt and direct manner of speaking and ability to cut through pretense and reveal the truth. He is also believed to be able to impart wisdom and guidance to those who seek his counsel. Baron Cimetière is honored during the Festival of the Dead in Haiti, which takes place in November. In New Orleans Voodoo, he is also celebrated during this time and during the annual Day of the Dead festivities in early November. At these events, offerings of rum, cigars, and black coffee are typically made to honor him, and his veve is often drawn on the ground or on a ceremonial altar.

Gede Nibo

Gede Nibo, the Loa of death and fertility in the Vodou tradition. Gede Nibo is a powerful and mischievous spirit with a sharp wit and a penchant for ribald humor. In the Vodou tradition, Nibo is often depicted as a skeletal figure adorned with a top hat, a black coat, a staff, and medicinal white rum. He is effeminate, too, frequently smoking a cigar. His veve, or sacred symbol, is a series of interconnected triangles representing the crossroads between life and death. Other symbols associated with this Lwa include coffins, bones, and the colors black and purple.

In Haitian Vodou, Gede Nibo is often syncretized with Saint Gerard Majella, a Christian saint known for bringing quick solutions to problems. In New Orleans Voodoo, Gede Nibo is often syncretized with Saint Martin de Porres, a Catholic saint known for his work with the poor and the sick. His correspondences include black and purple and the herbs basil, wormwood, and sage. He is often associated with cemeteries and crossroads and is said to have the power to bring fertility to those who honor him.

In the Vodou pantheon, Gede Nibo is closely related to the other Loa of death and the afterlife, including Baron Samedi and Maman Brigitte. He is also known for his close relationship with Papa Legba (the Loa), the gatekeeper between the mortal and spirit worlds. Gede Nibo is mischievous but also deeply powerful and wise. He is said to be able to see through the veil between life and death and uses his knowledge to help those seeking his guidance.

Legend tells of a young woman who was stricken with a serious illness. Her family called upon Gede Nibo for help, and he appeared to them as a skeleton carrying a cane and a top hat. He instructed the family to prepare a special offering of black coffee and rum and to place it at the crossroads. The family did as they were told, and he accepted their offering and healed the young woman, restoring her to full health.

Gede Nibo is also known for his love of music and dance and is often invoked during celebrations and festivals. One traditional dance that is associated with this spirit is the Banda dance, which involves a group of dancers moving in a circle while playing drums and other percussion instruments. In Haitian Vodou, Gede Nibo is often associated with the practice of ancestor veneration and is said to have the power to communicate with the spirits of the dead. Devotees may call upon Gede Nibo to help them connect with their ancestors and to seek their guidance and wisdom.

Preferred offerings for Gede Nibo include black coffee, rum, and cigars. Signs that he has received and accepted an offering may include the sudden appearance of a skeleton or a black dog or a sense of lightness and joy. Gede Nibo is celebrated and honored in New Orleans during the annual Vodou festival, Fet Gede, in late October or early November. During this festival, devotees offer gifts and perform rituals to honor Gede Nibo and the other Loa of death and the afterlife.

Gede Linto

This is a Lwa that is well known for making miracles happen. Like the rest of the Gede Lwa, he is all about death and fertility. Death isn't a bad thing when it comes to this family of Lwa, as it is simply a gateway to more life and part of the process of living. He is typically depicted as a dark man, about five feet tall, cane in hand, with glasses and an old-time black hat. It is said that he is one Gede Lwa who is particular about manners and is quite gentle. Some say he's a small, sweet boy known for his playful and mischievous nature and his love of candy and toys.

Gede Linto, when depicted as a young boy, is shown with curly hair and a playful smile. His veve, a symbol used in Vodou rituals to invoke the presence of a Loa, features a heart, a cross, and a lollipop. He is not syncretized with any saint in particular; still, he is considered a part of the Gede family of Loa, which is associated with death and the spirit world. He is said to be associated with the color pink and the herbs mint and cinnamon. He is known to have a particular fondness for candy and sweets, often offered to him during Vodou ceremonies. Linto's veve is like that of Lantor, with a cross with two circles on both sides and a heart beneath it.

Guede Masaka and Guede Oussou

Guede Masaka is associated with the color black. His veve often includes a skull, crossbones, and a heart. He is known for his ability to remove obstacles and provide protection. Guede Oussou is associated with purple, and his veve often includes a skull and crossbones with a snake. He is known for his association with the rainbow and is often called upon for his ability to bring good luck and prosperity. He is also known for his irreverent and mischievous nature and is often depicted as fond of alcohol and tobacco.

Guede Masaka and Guede Oussou are often referred to as "gravediggers" in Haitian Vodou. This is because they are believed to have the power to bury and exhume corpses. In Haitian Vodou, working with the dead is seen as a sacred and powerful skill, and both Guede are revered for their ability to navigate the realms of the dead. They are seen as powerful protectors and healers and are called upon for their ability to remove obstacles and provide spiritual guidance and support.

Guede Masaka and Guede Oussou are celebrated in Haitian Vodou during the annual Day of the Dead celebrations on November 1st and 2nd. During these celebrations, offerings of food, drink, and tobacco are made to the Guede, and they are honored and remembered as powerful and benevolent Lwa.

Gede Lantor

This Lwa is all about love and healing his devotees. What is interesting about him is that he is depicted as a woman with long, flowing hair. His correspondences include lightning and thunder, and he is known to assist anyone having issues with matters of the heart or sexuality. Lantor's veve looks like Linto's.

Chapter Six: The Petro Lwa

This chapter will discuss some of the most common Petro Lwa – so that you know everything there is to know about them! Knowing the Lwa will help you interact with them, make offerings, and more. It's easier to feel their presence in your life when you know who you're dealing with.

Simbi Andezo

Simbi Andezo is a water spirit in Haitian Vodou and New Orleans Voodoo. He is associated with the Simbi family of Loa; he is often depicted as a serpent, though he may also appear as a water snake or fish. He is known for his ability to grant knowledge, particularly of the secrets of the natural world, and for his healing powers.

His veve, or sacred symbol, typically includes a serpent or fish-like figure with a crescent moon and various other symbols representing water and knowledge. In Haitian Vodou, Simbi Andezo is often syncretized with Saint Patrick, while in New Orleans Voodoo, he may be associated with St. James the Greater or St. Dominic. His correspondences include blue and green and water-associated herbs such as basil, mint, and bay leaf.

Simbi Andezo has a close relationship with other members of the Simbi family of Loa and other water spirits, such as Agwe and La Sirene. In lore, he is often described as wise, knowledgeable, mischievous, and unpredictable. He enjoys offerings of rum, tobacco, and fish and may also appreciate gifts of knowledge, such as books or other educational materials. In Haitian Vodou, Simbi Andezo is celebrated on June 24th, the feast day of St. John the Baptist, also associated with water. In New Orleans Voodoo, he may be honored on June 29th, the feast day of St. Peter, who is also associated with water. In Hoodoo, he may be called upon for his knowledge and healing powers through spells and charms.

Gran Bwa

Gran Bwa, the powerful Loa of the forest, is a force to be reckoned with in Haitian Vodou, New Orleans Voodoo, and Hoodoo. This ancient spirit has deep roots, and his influence is felt far and wide. In appearance, Gran Bwa is often depicted as a towering figure with a fierce and formidable presence. He is said to wear a hat made of leaves and be draped in foliage, symbolizing his deep connection to the natural world. His visage is often carved into totems and sculptures, and his image is used in veves, and other sacred symbols associated with his worship.

Regarding symbols, Gran Bwa's veve is a powerful image representing his essence and energy. It is a swirling, intricate pattern of lines and curves that is said to embody the spirit of the forest and the power of nature. His other associated symbols include trees, leaves, and various other flora and fauna found in the wilderness. While Gran Bwa is not syncretized with any particular saint, he is often associated with Saint Sebastian, a Christian martyr known for his deep devotion and unwavering faith. It is said that Gran Bwa shares many of these qualities and is a protector of the faithful.

Gran Bwa's correspondences include the colors green and brown, which are associated with the natural world and the forest. His preferred herbs and plants include basil, patchouli, and cedar, which have strong protective and purifying properties. His associations with the forest mean he is also closely linked to the animals that inhabit it, including the serpent, the owl, and the bear. Regarding his relationships with other Loa, Gran Bwa is known to be a solitary figure and often seen as a guardian or protector of the other spirits. His fierce and protective nature means that the other Loa deeply respect him, and his powers are often called upon during times of danger or strife.

Lore connected to Gran Bwa depicts him as a powerful and sometimes unpredictable force that must be treated with great respect and reverence. He is said to be wise and knowledgeable but also capable of great anger and retribution if his boundaries are crossed, or his sacred spaces are violated. Despite his fearsome reputation, however, he is also known to be a kind and caring protector, particularly of children and those who are vulnerable. Offerings to Gran Bwa often include offerings of food, drink, sacred herbs, and plants. He is particularly fond of rum, and offerings of this potent spirit are said to be especially pleasing. Signs that he has received and accepted an offering can include a sudden gust of wind, the rustling of leaves, or the appearance of an animal or bird associated with the forest.

In Haitian Vodou, New Orleans Voodoo, and Hoodoo, Gran Bwa is celebrated and honored in various ways. Offerings are made at altars dedicated to him, and his veve is drawn on the ground to summon his power and presence. Special ceremonies are also held in his honor, particularly during the Feast of Saint Sebastian, associated with his worship.

Ti Jean Petro

Ti Jean Petro is a powerful Loa in Haitian Vodou, known for his trickster nature, fierce energy, and connection to fire. Like many Loas, his appearance and personality can vary depending on the context and the worshiper's relationship with him. In some depictions, he is said to be a short, muscular man with a wild mane of hair, often wearing a red scarf or bandanna around his head. He is sometimes shown carrying a machete, a symbol of his warrior spirit, and may also be depicted with a serpent or a black rooster, both associated with his energy and power. The veve of Ti-Jean Petro is a complex and ornate design, featuring interlocking circles and a central image of a human figure with outstretched arms. Other associated symbols include the sun, a rooster, and red and black, representing his fiery and passionate nature. He is often syncretized with St. James the Greater, a Christian saint associated with war and battle. This connection highlights his fierce and protective energy and his ability to provide strength and courage to his followers.

Regarding correspondence, Ti Jean Petro is associated with the color red and plants and herbs such as hot peppers, ginger, and tobacco. His energy is said to be connected to fire and heat, and he is often called upon to provide protection, strength, and power in difficult situations. This spirit is closely connected with other Loas in the Vodou pantheon, particularly those associated with the Petro tradition, emphasizing fiery and aggressive energy. He is often associated with other powerful and intense Loas, such as Ezili Dantor, Papa Legba, and Baron Samedi, with whom he shares a connection to death and the underworld.

Lore surrounding Ti Jean Petro often emphasizes his trickster nature and his ability to outwit and manipulate others. He is said to enjoy playing pranks and tricks but also has a deeply compassionate and protective side, particularly for vulnerable or oppressed people. Offerings to this spirit may include red candles, spicy foods, and alcohol, as well as items such as knives, machetes, or other tools associated with his warrior energy. Signs that he has accepted an offering may include a feeling of heat or intense energy and sightings of roosters or other symbols associated with his energy. Ti Jean Petro is celebrated and honored in various ways throughout the Vodou tradition, particularly in the Petro tradition. His feast day is July 25th, typically marked by feasting, dancing, and other celebrations in his honor. In New Orleans Voodoo and Hoodoo, Ti Jean Petro is sometimes called "Papa Jean." He is often associated with the color red and with fiery, protective energy. He may be invoked in spells and rituals related to courage, strength, and overcoming obstacles.

Carrefour

Carrefour is a powerful and enigmatic Loa in Haitian Vodou, New Orleans Voodoo, and Hoodoo traditions. He is associated with crossroads, transitions, and change and is often called upon to bring luck, protection, and guidance. Depicted as a tall, thin man with dark skin, dressed in ragged clothes and carrying a cane, Carrefour is sometimes shown with a skull on his hat or necklace, symbolizing death and the crossing between worlds. His veve, or ritual symbol, is a complex pattern of interlocking triangles and circles, representing the intersections of paths and the power of change.

In Haitian Vodou, Carrefour is often syncretized with Saint Peter, the Christian apostle, and keeper of the keys to heaven. This connection reflects his role as a guardian of gateways and thresholds, both physical and spiritual. In New Orleans Voodoo, he is sometimes associated with Papa Legba, another Loa associated with crossroads and gatekeeping. His correspondences include black and red, representing death and life, respectively. His associated plants include horehound, tobacco, and cypress; his offerings may include rum, cigars, and chicken. He is also known to enjoy hot peppers and spicy foods, which represent his fiery nature.

In Haitian Vodou, Carrefour is often considered a powerful and feared Loa, associated with danger and chaos. He is known to be a trickster and a master of illusion and is said to be able to grant both blessings and curses. Despite this reputation, however, he is revered for his ability to bring about change and transformation and is sometimes called upon to help with legal or financial matters. In New Orleans Voodoo and Hoodoo, Carrefour is sometimes known as Papa La Bas and is associated with the city's historic Congo Square, a gathering place for enslaved Africans and their descendants. In these traditions, he is often called upon to protect the community and provide guidance during times of change and upheaval.

To honor and work with Carrefour, practitioners may create a sacred space with his veve and offer him appropriate offerings, such as rum, tobacco, or spicy foods. Signs that he has received and accepted an offering may include the appearance of black or red birds or the scent of cigar smoke. Carrefour is celebrated and honored in various ways throughout the year, including on January 6th, the feast day of Saint Peter, and during the Haitian Vodou festivals of Fet Gede and Fet Nago. In New Orleans Voodoo and Hoodoo traditions, he may be honored during Mardi Gras and other celebrations that emphasize crossing boundaries and the transformation of the self.

Ezili Gé Rouge

Ezili Gé Rouge, the "Red-Eyed Lady," is a powerful and complex Lwa in Haitian Vodou. She is often associated with love, beauty, passion, and sensuality but also with war, fire, and destruction. In her visual representation, this Lwa is often depicted as a beautiful woman with piercing red eyes dressed in red and black clothing. She may wear a crown of thorns or have a snake wrapped around her neck. Her veve, or sacred symbol, features a heart with an arrow through it, surrounded by flames. While she is not syncretized with a Catholic saint, some practitioners may associate her with Saint Barbara or Saint Catherine.

Ezili Gé Rouge's correspondences include the colors red and black, the herbs vervain and dragon's blood, and the flowers hibiscus and red roses. She is associated with fire, lightning, and the element of air. She may be invoked alongside other Ezili spirits like Ezili Dantor and Ezili Freda. She is also said to have connections to the Lwa Ogou and Agwe. Lore surrounding Ezili Gé Rouge often depicts her as a powerful and passionate figure, quick to anger but also fiercely protective of her devotees. She is seen as a force to be reckoned with, capable of great love and destruction.

Offerings to this Lwa may include red wine, red candles, spicy foods, and perfume. Devotees may also offer her blood, which is not recommended for inexperienced practitioners. Signs that she has received and accepted an offering may include strong winds, sudden flames, or the scent of burning roses. Ezili Gé Rouge is honored in Haitian Vodou through private and public ceremonies, often held on Fridays. Although practices may differ, she may also be celebrated in New Orleans Voodoo and Hoodoo traditions. Her devotees may dance, sing, and offer offerings in her honor, seeking her protection, guidance, and blessings in matters of love, relationships, and passion.

Ezili Dantor

Ezili Dantor, the Haitian Vodou goddess of love, motherhood, and protection, is a powerful and revered figure in the pantheon of Loa. Her image is that of a fierce and protective mother, often depicted with a child in her arms, a machete in one hand, and a fiery torch in the other. She is known to be both nurturing and fiercely protective, fiercely loyal to her children, and unafraid to defend them against any threat. Her veve is a depiction of a heart pierced by a sword, surrounded by the letters of her name. She is syncretized with the Catholic figure of the Black Madonna, and her colors are typically red and blue. Her correspondences include the herbs basil, rue, vervain, and the plants rose and hibiscus. She is associated with the number 9; her favorite foods are pork, eggplant, and bread.

Ezili Dantor is known to have close relationships with other Loa, including Ogou, the god of war, and Erzili Freda, the goddess of love and beauty. She is often seen as a protector of women and children and is also associated with lesbianism and same-sex relationships. According to lore, she is a fierce and protective mother figure who will go to great lengths to defend her children. One story tells of her using her machete to cut off her head and offer it to the spirit of her daughter, who had been captured and enslaved by white plantation owners.

Preferred offerings to Ezili Dantor include red and blue candles, flowers, and sweet-smelling oils. Signs that she has received and accepted an offering can include the smell of sweet perfume or flowers and a feeling of warmth or comfort. Ezili Dantor is celebrated and honored in Haitian Vodou, New Orleans Voodoo, and Hoodoo. In Haitian Vodou, she is often associated with the Petwo rites, known for their intense and fiery energy. Her feast day is celebrated on May 30th, and offerings are made at her altars in hopes of gaining her protection and blessings.

In New Orleans Voodoo and Hoodoo, she is often associated with the figure of Marie Laveau, the famous Voodoo queen who was said to have worshipped Ezili Dantor. Her image can be found in many Voodoo and Hoodoo shops, and offerings are made to her in hopes of gaining her assistance in matters of love, protection, and fertility. In all of her incarnations, Ezili Dantor is a powerful and revered figure known for her fierce love and unwavering protection. She is a symbol of strength and resilience and a reminder that even in the face of great adversity, we can find the courage and fortitude to overcome.

Agwe La Flambeau

Agwe La Flambeau is a powerful and respected Loa in Haitian Vodou, New Orleans Voodoo, and Hoodoo traditions. He is the spirit of the sea and is associated with water, the ocean, and all aquatic life. This Lwa is often depicted as a strong and muscular man with skin as dark as the ocean depths. He wears a long blue coat and a captain's hat, symbolizing his command over the vast expanse of the sea. His veve is a complex symbol that incorporates a variety of marine life, including fish, seashells, and waves. It is often drawn in white or blue powder and is used in ceremonies to call upon his energy and power. Other symbols associated with Agwe include boats, anchors, and tridents.

In some syncretic traditions, Agwe is associated with Saint Ulrich, who is revered in some areas of Haiti as the patron saint of seafarers. However, he is not syncretized to any particular saint in other traditions. He is associated with the color blue, representing the ocean and the depths of the sea. His sacred plants include seaweed, sea grape, and sea lavender. Offerings to him often include seafood, such as fish, crab, or lobster, as well as blue candles and blue flowers.

Agwe is closely associated with other water spirits like La Sirène and Simbi. He is also believed to work closely with the Gede, the spirits of the dead, in ceremonies taking place on the water. All the tales about this Lwa depict him as a powerful and benevolent spirit who is fiercely protective of those who call upon him. He is known to calm even the roughest of seas and provide safe passage for those who travel on the water. In some stories, Agwe is also associated with wealth and prosperity, as he is believed to control the ocean's vast resources. Signs that he has accepted an offering may include an increase in the strength of the ocean currents or the appearance of dolphins or other marine life near a boat. Offerings may also be marked by the appearance of a blue flame, which is believed to be a sign of his presence.

Agwe is celebrated and honored in various ceremonies and rituals in Haitian Vodou, New Orleans Voodoo, and Hoodoo. In some traditions, he is honored on the feast day of Saint Ulrich, while in others, he has his own dedicated ceremonies. Many ceremonies dedicated to this spirit take place on the water, with offerings made to him at the sea's edge or on boats sent out into the open ocean. These ceremonies often involve music, dance, and drumming to call upon Agwe's power and honor his role as the spirit of the sea.

Ogun Petro

Ogun Petro is a powerful and dynamic Loa in Haitian Vodou, with a fiery personality and a strong presence that commands respect. He is associated with fire, iron, and metalworking and is often depicted as a blacksmith, wielding his hammer and anvil with strength and skill. In his human form, this Lwa is often described as tall and muscular, with dark skin and piercing eyes that seem to glow with the intensity of the flames he commands. He wears a red or black hat and a red or white scarf around his neck, sometimes adorned with a necklace of iron or other metals. The veve of Ogun Petro is a complex and powerful symbol, often featuring a central image of a hammer and anvil, surrounded by fiery symbols and other motifs associated with metalworking and the forge. It is said that his veve has the power to open doorways and summon his spirit, so it is treated with great reverence and respect by practitioners of Haitian Vodou.

Ogun Petro is syncretized with the Catholic saint, St. James the Greater, who is often depicted as a warrior or a pilgrim, wielding a sword and wearing a hat adorned with scallop shells. This association with St. James reflects Lwa's reputation as a powerful and fierce protector of his followers, who will stop at nothing to defend them from harm and injustice. In terms of his correspondences, Ogun Petro is associated with the color red and iron, steel, and other metals. He is also associated with herbs and plants such as basil, rue, and tobacco, which are often used in offerings and rituals dedicated to him.

Ogun is known for his close relationships with other powerful Loa, including Ezili Dantor, Baron Samedi, and Papa Legba. He is particularly close to the fiery Loa known as Met Kalfou, with whom he shares a powerful bond based on their shared association with fire and the forge. This iron Lwa is often depicted as a fierce and unyielding warrior, willing to take on any challenge or foe to protect his people. He is often associated with acts of bravery and heroism and is seen as a symbol of strength, determination, and courage in the face of adversity.

Preferred offerings to Ogun Petro include offerings of meat, rum, and other strong spirits, as well as metal objects such as knives, tools, or even automobile parts. Signs that he has received and accepted one's offerings may include the flickering of flames or the sound of metal clanging in the distance. Ogun Petro is often honored through fiery ceremonies involving bonfires, sparks, and the pounding of metal. These celebrations may occur at specific times of the year, such as the Feast of St. James in July, or they may be held in honor of specific events or occasions. In New Orleans Voodoo and Hoodoo, Ogun Petro is often associated with the powerful ritual of "cutting and clearing," which involves using metal tools to clear away negative energy and obstacles in one's life.

Chapter Seven: Voodoo and Hoodoo Altars

Do You Need a Shrine or an Altar?

In the practice of Voodoo and Hoodoo, an altar or shrine can be a powerful tool used to connect with the spiritual world. It serves as a focal point for your devotion, gives a space for your offerings, and is a dedicated place for your prayers. But the question remains. Is an altar or shrine necessary?

A voodoo shrine.

Calvin Hennick, for WBUR Boston, CC BY 3.0 <https://creativecommons.org/licenses/by/3.0>,
via Wikimedia Commons
*https://commons.wikimedia.org/wiki/File:Haitian_vodou_altar_to_Petwo,_Rada,_and_Gede_spir
its;_November_5,_2010..jpg*

The answer to this question is both yes and no. It ultimately depends on your personal beliefs and practices. For some, an altar is an essential part of their spiritual practice. For others, it is not necessary. Suppose you find comfort and connection in having a physical space for your spiritual practice. In that case, an altar can be a powerful tool. You can use your altar to honor your ancestors, deities, or saints. You can also use it to create a space for your prayers, to offer thanks, or to seek guidance.

The act of setting up an altar can be a meditative and intentional process. You can choose items that have personal significance to you, such as candles, crystals, statues, or pictures. You can also use items that are traditionally associated with Voodoo and Hoodoo, such as graveyard dirt, red brick dust, or mojo bags. Your altar can be as simple or elaborate as you like. It can be a small corner of your room or an entire room dedicated to your practice. The key is to create a space that feels sacred to you, a space that allows you to connect with the spiritual world in a meaningful way.

But what if you are someone who does not feel the need for an altar or shrine or who, for some reason, cannot set one up? Is it still possible to connect with the spiritual world without one? The answer is yes. You do not need a physical space to connect with the spiritual world. You can connect with the divine through your thoughts, actions, and intentions. You can offer prayers and thanks wherever you are, whether you are in a crowded city or a quiet forest. Do not feel discouraged if you do not have the space or resources to create an altar. There are many ways to connect with the spiritual world without one. You can create a virtual altar using images and symbols that resonate with you. You can also simply take a moment each day to reflect on your spirituality, offer thanks, or ask for guidance.

Ultimately, whether or not you choose to have an altar or shrine is a personal decision. It is important to honor your beliefs and practices and create a spiritual practice that *feels authentic.* Whether you create a physical space for your practice or connect with the spiritual world in other ways, know that your intentions and devotion truly matter. In Voodoo and Hoodoo, the most important aspect of your practice is your connection to the spiritual world. Whether you choose to have an altar or not, the key is approaching your practice with reverence and respect. The spiritual world is a powerful and sacred place, and it is up to you to create a practice that honors its complexity and beauty.

If you choose to create an altar or shrine, there are several considerations to remember. First, choosing a location that feels sacred to you is important. This may be a corner of your room, a dedicated space in your home, or even a space outside. The key is to choose a location that feels comfortable and conducive to your spiritual practice. Second, choosing items that are personally significant to you is important. This may include candles, crystals, statues, or pictures. You may also choose items traditionally associated with Voodoo and Hoodoo, such as graveyard dirt, red brick dust, or mojo bags. The items you choose should be meaningful to you and help you connect with the spiritual world personally and authentically.

Third, it is important to set intentions for your altar or shrine. What do you hope to achieve through your practice? With whom do you hope to connect? Setting intentions allows you to create a focused and intentional practice that helps you achieve your spiritual goals. Finally, it is important to maintain your altar or shrine with care and respect. Keep it clean and organized, and refresh your offerings regularly. Take time each day to connect with your altar and to offer your prayers and thanks.

How to Create a Voodoo Altar for a Lwa

Creating a Voodoo altar dedicated to a specific Lwa can be a powerful and transformative experience. An altar can serve as a physical space for you to connect with the spiritual world and deepen your relationship with a specific Lwa. In this guide, you'll get some useful ideas on creating a Voodoo altar dedicated to a specific Lwa and some tips on how to honor and connect with your chosen Lwa.

Step One — Choosing your Lwa: First, choosing a Lwa to which you feel a strong connection is important. The Lwa are spirits that serve as intermediaries between the human and divine worlds. Each Lwa has its own personality, energy, and areas of influence. Some of the most well-known Lwa include Papa Legba, Baron Samedi, Ezili Danto, and Ogun. Research and explore the different Lwa to find one that resonates with you.

Step Two — Choosing and cleansing the space: Once you have chosen a Lwa, it is time to create your altar. Find a space in your home that feels sacred, and that can be dedicated to your practice. You can use a small table, a shelf, or even a corner of your room. Cleanse the space with some sage or incense to clear any negative energy and create a sacred atmosphere.

Step Three — Choosing what goes on your altar: Next, choose some items associated with your chosen Lwa to place on your altar. These may include candles, herbs, crystals, statues, or other symbolic items. For example, suppose you are creating an altar for Papa Legba. In that case, you may choose to place a statue of him on your altar, along with a white candle, some tobacco, and some rum. Suppose you are creating an altar for Ezili Danto. In that case, you may choose to place a statue of her on your altar, along with some red candles, some roses, and some champagne.

When placing your items on the altar, consider the energy and symbolism of each item. Each item should have a specific purpose and intention. For example, candles can represent the light and energy of the divine, while herbs can be used for protection and healing. Choose items that feel meaningful to you and that help you connect with the energy of your chosen Lwa.

Step Four — Connecting with your Lwa: Once you have set up your altar, it is time to connect with your chosen Lwa. One way to do this is through prayer and offerings. Light a candle and some incense, and offer some food or drink to your Lwa. Speak to your Lwa from your heart, and ask for their guidance and protection. You may also choose to perform a ritual or a dance to honor your Lwa and deepen your connection.

Another way to connect with your chosen Lwa is through meditation and visualization. Sit in front of your altar and close your eyes. Visualize your chosen Lwa standing in front of you, and imagine yourself surrounded by their energy and protection. Allow yourself to be open to any messages or guidance your Lwa may offer.

Step Five — Caring for your altar: Maintaining your altar with care and respect is important. Keep it clean and organized, and refresh your offerings regularly. Take time each day to connect with your altar and to offer your prayers and thanks.

Switching Your Voodoo Altar to a Hoodoo One

Changing your Voodoo altar to a Hoodoo one can be a meaningful transformation in your spiritual practice. Hoodoo is a form of African

American folk magic closely related to Voodoo but has unique traditions and practices. If you are interested in incorporating Hoodoo into your practice, you can do a few things to change your Voodoo altar to a Hoodoo one.

First, it is important to understand the differences between Voodoo and Hoodoo. While both traditions share some commonalities, Hoodoo is often more focused on practical magic and spellwork, while Voodoo focuses more on spiritual connection and ritual. Hoodoo also emphasizes the use of herbs, roots, and other natural materials in spellwork.

To change your Voodoo altar to a Hoodoo one, add some Hoodoo-specific items to your altar. These may include herbs, roots, oils, and other ingredients commonly used in Hoodoo spells. You can also add some symbolic items, such as a mojo bag or a small mirror, often used in Hoodoo magic.

Another way to change your Voodoo altar to a Hoodoo one is to incorporate some specific Hoodoo rituals and practices into your daily routine. For example, you can perform a daily spiritual bath or use a specific oil to anoint yourself before spellwork. You can also incorporate some specific prayers or chants associated with Hoodoo.

Setting Up Your Altar for Ancestral Veneration

If you are interested in ancestral veneration, you can also change your altar to make it suitable for this practice. Ancestral veneration is the practice of honoring and connecting with your ancestors, who are seen as powerful spiritual guides and protectors. Here are some helpful tips for creating an ancestral veneration altar:

Incorporate their photos: Incorporating photos or portraits of your ancestors on your altar can be a powerful way to visually connect with them during your worship. When you place a photo of your ancestor or ancestors on your altar, it serves as a reminder of their presence in your life and their relevance to your family history. It can be a way to honor their memory and acknowledge their contributions to your life and the lives of your ancestors. Photos of your ancestors on your altar can also help create a sacred space for you to connect with them. When you sit down to worship at your altar, seeing the faces of your ancestors can create a sense of comfort and familiarity. It can help you to feel less alone and more connected to your family history and ancestry.

Furthermore, incorporating photos of your ancestors can be a way to keep their memory alive. As time passes, it can be easy to forget the details of your family history and your ancestors' stories. However, by displaying their photos on your altar, you keep their memory alive and preserve their legacy for future generations. When choosing which photos to display on your altar, you may want to consider selecting images that are meaningful to you or represent significant moments in your family's history. For example, you may choose a photo of your great-grandmother on her wedding day or a photo of your grandfather during his military service. You may also choose to display photos of ancestors who have passed away more recently to honor their memory and keep their spirits close.

Additionally, it is important to treat the photos of your ancestors with respect and care. You may want to consider framing or placing them in protective sleeves to prevent damage or deterioration over time. You may also want to periodically clean the photos or arrange them in a way that feels aesthetically pleasing to you.

Use the items that they once owned: These items could be anything with personal significance or sentimental value, such as jewelry, clothing, or other heirlooms. Placing these items on your altar creates a tangible connection to your family history and ancestors. When you see and touch these items, you can connect with your ancestors in a more visceral way. It can be a powerful experience to hold something your ancestor once owned or wore and feel you are a part of their legacy.

Placing these items on your altar can also serve as a way to honor the memory of your ancestors and respect their contributions to your family history. For example, you may display a piece of jewelry passed down through several generations of your family or a garment your great-grandmother hand-sewed. These items can remind you of the sacrifices and hard work that your ancestors put into building your family legacy. When placing these items on your altar, it is important to treat them carefully. You could consider placing them on a special cloth or display stand or arranging them in a way that feels aesthetically pleasing to you. You may also want to clean the items periodically to prevent damage or deterioration.

Offer them their favorite food and drink: This can be a powerful way to honor their memory and create a sense of connection with them through shared experiences and traditions. Offering food or drink to your ancestors can be done in various ways. One approach is to offer something significant to them during their life. For example, suppose your grandmother loved a particular type of tea. In that case, you could offer that tea on your altar as a way to connect with her and honor her memory. Similarly, if your grandfather had a favorite food or drink, you could consider offering that item on your altar in his honor.

Another approach is to prepare a special dish or beverage aimed specifically at your ancestors' memory. This could be a family recipe passed down through the generations or a dish you create based on your ancestors' cultural traditions. By preparing this food or drink and offering it on your altar, you are creating a sense of continuity with your family history and honoring the traditions and customs of your ancestors. When offering food or drink on your altar, it is important to do so with care and respect. You might choose to place the food or drink on a special plate or cup or arrange it in a way that feels aesthetically pleasing to you. You may also want to light candles or incense to further honor your ancestors and create a sacred space for their memory.

Frequently Asked Questions

Q: Is it okay to have multiple altars?

A: Yes, it is absolutely okay to have multiple altars. In fact, many practitioners have separate altars for different purposes, such as one for ancestors, one for Lwas, and one for other spiritual beings. Having multiple altars allows you to focus your energy on specific practice areas. It can help you create a more personalized and meaningful spiritual practice.

Q: If I dedicate an altar to both an ancestor and a Lwa, would that be fine?

A: It is perfectly fine to dedicate an altar to an ancestor and a Lwa. In Voodoo, ancestors and Lwas are often seen as interconnected, and it is not uncommon for practitioners to honor both on the same altar. Just follow any specific rituals or practices associated with each spirit and show them both the respect they deserve.

Q: May I dedicate my altar to several Lwas?

A: Yes, it is possible to dedicate your altar to multiple Lwas, although it is important to do so with care and respect. Before dedicating your altar to multiple Lwas, make sure that you understand each Lwa's characteristics and requirements and that you can provide the necessary offerings and attention to each spirit. For instance, you should never have the same altar for a Rada and a Petro Lwa unless you've partitioned the altar so that one half is dedicated to each nanchon.

Q: What should I do with the food offerings after a while?

A: It is important to dispose of food offerings respectfully. In many Voodoo traditions, it is common to leave offerings out for a certain period (such as 24 hours) and then dispose of them naturally, such as burying them in the earth or throwing them into running water. Be sure to do so in a way that is respectful to the spirits and to the environment.

Q: How do I cleanse the altar?

A: Cleansing the altar is important to maintaining a spiritual practice. Depending on your specific tradition and preferences, there are many ways to cleanse an altar. One common method is to use smoke from herbs or incense, such as sage or palo santo. You can also use sounds like a bell or a singing bowl to clear negative energy. Another approach is to physically clean the altar with water and mild soap while focusing on the intention of cleansing and purifying the space. Whatever method you choose, be sure to do so with care and intention, and always show respect for the spirits and the altar itself.

Q: Can I use my altar for divination or spellwork?

A: Altars can be used for various spiritual practices, including divination and spellwork. However, it is important to approach these practices with care and respect and to follow any specific rituals or traditions associated with them. If you are new to divination or spellwork, it would be helpful to seek guidance from a more experienced practitioner or to extensively research and practice before attempting these spiritual practices on your own.

Q: How often should I clean and refresh my altar?

A: The frequency with which you clean and refresh your altar will depend on your specific practice and the spirits with which you are working. Some practitioners prefer to clean their altar daily or weekly, while others may only do so on special occasions or when working with specific spirits. It is important to listen to your intuition and the guidance of the spirits when it comes to maintaining your altar. You should always show respect and care for the space used and the spirits you are working with.

Q: What should I do if my altar is disturbed or damaged?

A: If your altar is disturbed or damaged in any way, it is important to take the necessary steps to restore it as soon as possible. The first thing you should do is assess the extent of the damage. If it is minor, you may be able to repair it yourself. You may need to consult a spiritual practitioner or elder for guidance if it is more extensive. Regardless of the extent of the damage, it is important to cleanse and re-consecrate the altar after it has been repaired. This can be done by smudging the area with sage or palo santo, anointing the altar with holy water or Florida water, and offering prayers and offerings to the spirits to ask for their forgiveness and blessings. It is also important to investigate the cause of the disturbance or damage. If it was due to natural causes such as a storm or earthquake, you might need to perform a special ritual to appease the spirits of the land. If it was due to human interference, you might need to perform a more involved ritual to remove any negative energy and protect your altar from future harm.

Chapter Eight: Mojo Bags and Gris-Gris

Mojo bags and gris-gris are among the most important Voodoo charms, even though most people seem to know only about Voodoo dolls which are actually a form of gris-gris on their own. In this chapter, you'll learn everything about these charms and their uses, as well as how to make them.

A mojo bag.
Teogomez, CC BY-SA 3.0 <http://creativecommons.org/licenses/by-sa/3.0/>, via Wikimedia Commons https://commons.wikimedia.org/wiki/File:Grisgristuareg.JPG

Gris-Gris? Mojo Bags?

Mojo bags and gris-gris are powerful charms rooted in Voodoo beliefs and practices. These objects are more than mere trinkets. They are imbued with spiritual power and meaning and are integral to the Voodoo tradition. Sometimes they're known as monjo or jomo bags. Mojo bags are small, usually flannel or leather pouches filled with herbs, roots, stones, and other magical ingredients. They are often carried on by the person or can be placed in a specific location, such as on an altar or in a sacred space.

Gris-gris, on the other hand, is more specific to the New Orleans Voodoo tradition. The word "gris-gris" is believed to come from the Yoruba word for juju. Some say it's from the French word "*joujou*," which refers to a plaything or toy. Gris-gris are also bags filled with magical ingredients, but they are usually worn on a string around the neck or waist. Gris-gris can also be used in other forms, such as small cloth dolls, totems, or even powders.

Both mojo bags and gris-gris are deeply connected to Voodoo beliefs and practices. In the Voodoo tradition, everything in the universe is believed to be imbued with spiritual energy. This energy can be harnessed and used for various purposes, from healing to protection to love spells. Mojo bags and gris-gris are tools that Voodoo practitioners use to access this energy and channel it toward a specific goal. In Voodoo, the ingredients that go into mojo bags and gris-gris are carefully chosen for their spiritual properties. For example, herbs like basil, rosemary, and mint are believed to have protective qualities, while roots like mandrake, sarsaparilla, and ginseng are thought to have healing powers. Stones like amethyst, quartz, and hematite are believed to have different energies, used for different purposes.

How mojo bags and gris-gris are made and used also reflects Voodoo beliefs and practices. These charms are often made during specific phases of the moon or during certain times of the year when the spiritual energy is believed to be particularly strong. The person making the charm may also perform specific rituals or prayers to imbue it with additional power. The uses of mojo bags and gris-gris are as varied as the ingredients that go into them. They can be used for protection, luck, love, money, and even to curse an enemy. In some cases, they may be combined with other Voodoo practices, such as candle magic or spiritual baths.

In Voodoo, mojo bags and gris-gris are considered to be very personal objects. They are often made specifically for an individual and may even contain personal items like hair or fingernail clippings. It is believed that the closer the connection between the individual and the charm, the more powerful it will be.

How to Make Your Mojo Bag

Creating a mojo bag is a sacred ritual that requires care and attention. Before beginning, choosing the right materials and setting your intentions is important. A mojo bag is a personal item; each should be crafted with love and care. To make a mojo bag, you will need the following materials:

- A small piece of cloth or bag made from natural materials (such as cotton, silk, or leather)
- Herbs, roots, or other natural ingredients (such as bones, crystals, or coins) which correspond to your intention
- Thread or string
- Scissors
- Anointing oil (optional)

Now that you have gathered your materials, it is time to begin:

1. **Set your intention:** Before you start, it's important to set your intention. Decide what you want your mojo bag to do for you. For example, do you want it to bring you love, success, or protection? This intention will guide your selection of materials.

2. **Choose your ingredients:** Select herbs, roots, or other natural items which correspond with your intention. Consider consulting the plant and herb symbolism guide in the previous chapter of this book for guidance.

3. **Cut the cloth:** Cut a small square of cloth, or use a pre-made bag large enough to hold your ingredients.

4. **Add your ingredients**: Place your chosen ingredients inside the bag or on the cloth. *Be careful to choose only those items which correspond to your intention.* For example, if you want to attract love, you may use rose petals, cinnamon, and catnip. If you want protection, you could use a piece of hematite, sage, and a pinch of salt.

5. **Tie the bag:** After adding ingredients, carefully tie up the bag or cloth using the string or thread. As you tie the bag, focus on your intention, and ask for the blessings of the spirits and ancestors.

6. **Anoint the bag (optional):** You can anoint your bag with an oil corresponding to your intention. For example, if you want to attract love, you could use rose oil. You could use a protective oil such as frankincense if you want protection.

7. **Personalize the bag:** Your mojo bag should be a personal item that reflects your individual spirit. You can personalize it by adding a small talisman or charm representing you or something important to you. This could be a piece of jewelry or a small trinket.

8. **Consecrate the bag:** You should consecrate your mojo bag by placing it on your altar and asking for the blessings of the spirits and ancestors. You can also cleanse it in the smoke of burned incense or sage to eliminate any negative energy.

9. **Breathe on the bag:** Exhale through your mouth thrice onto the bag. This will activate it so it can get to work on the intention you set for it.

By following these steps, you can create a powerful and effective mojo bag imbued with the energy of your intentions and the blessings of your spirits and ancestors. Remember to treat your mojo bag with respect and care, and always keep it close to you for maximum effectiveness.

How to Make Your Gris-Gris

Making a gris-gris is a sacred and deeply personal practice in Voodoo. It involves choosing materials with specific meanings and intentions and creating a unique charm representing your desires and needs. To begin, gather the following materials:

- A piece of fabric, preferably red or black
- Needle and thread
- Herbs and spices, such as basil, cinnamon, or mint
- Small crystals or stones, such as clear quartz or black tourmaline
- Personal items, such as hair or nail clippings

• Paper and pen

• A charm or talisman, such as a small piece of jewelry or a coin

Once you have gathered your materials, follow these steps to create your gris-gris:

1. **Choose your intention**: Before you begin, it is important to know what you want to achieve with your gris-gris. Take some time to reflect on your desires and write them down on a piece of paper.

2. **Choose your materials**: Each herb, crystal, and personal item has its own meaning and energy. Choose items that align with your intention and add them to your work area.

3. **Cut your fabric:** Cut a small piece of fabric into a square or rectangle. The size of the fabric will depend on the size of your charm.

4. **Write your intention:** Using a pen or marker, write your intention on a small piece of paper. Fold the paper and place it in the center of the fabric.

5. **Add your herbs and spices:** Sprinkle a small number of herbs and spices onto the fabric. Each herb and spice has its own meaning, so choose ones that align with your intention. Fold the fabric over and sew the edges together, creating a small pouch.

6. **Add your crystals and personal items:** Add your crystals and personal items to the pouch. These items will add personal energy to your gris-gris and help align it with your intention.

7. **Add your charm:** Choose a charm or talisman representing your intention and add it to the pouch. This could be a small piece of jewelry or a coin.

8. **Close your gris-gris:** Once you have added all of your materials, close your gris-gris by tying it with a piece of thread. You can also sew it closed if you prefer.

9. **Cleanse and charge your gris-gris:** Hold it in your hands and focus your intention on it. You can also cleanse and charge it by placing it in the moonlight or smudging it with sage or palo santo.

10. **Breathe on the gris-gris**: Doing this will set it to work on whatever you made it for.

Remember, creating a gris-gris is a personal and sacred practice. Choose materials that align with your intention and trust your intuition. Look at the glossary at the end of the book for more ideas on what sort of materials you could use, as well as their spiritual meanings, so you can get more creative with your craft. May your mojo bag and gris-gris bring you the blessings and protection you seek!

Uses of Voodoo Charms

Protection: Mojo bags and gris-gris can be used for protection from negative energies, bad luck, and harm. Regarding voodoo practices, protection is one of the most common uses for mojo bags and gris-gris. These voodoo charms are believed to provide spiritual and physical protection against negative energies, bad luck, and harm.

In voodoo, protection is not just about physical safety but also about spiritual well-being. It is believed that negative energies and influences can attach to a person, causing emotional and mental distress. Mojo bags and gris-gris are thought to protect against these negative energies and help the person use them to maintain a sense of spiritual and emotional balance.

Love and relationships: Voodoo charms can attract or enhance love and strengthen relationships. Voodoo charms can also be used to bring harmony into relationships and deepen the connection between partners. Love and relationship charms can be made using various ingredients and symbols believed to have properties associated with love, passion, and romance. Symbols can be used in love and relationship charms. For example, a charm can be made using two interlocking hearts to represent a couple's love for each other. One or both partners can carry the charm to strengthen the bond between them. Other symbols that can be used include Cupid's arrow, which represents the power of love and attraction, and the infinity symbol, which represents the everlasting nature of love.

Using love and relationship charms can help to bring more love and harmony into your life. By focusing your energy and intentions on attracting love or enhancing your relationship, you can create positive energy to draw more love and happiness into your life. It is important to remember that love charms are not a substitute for healthy communication and actions in relationships but rather a tool to support and enhance the love that already exists.

Health and healing: Mojo bags and gris-gris can be used for physical, emotional, and spiritual healing. They can be powerful tools to promote physical, emotional, and spiritual healing. These charms can help alleviate ailments and provide strength and protection during illness. The materials used in creating these charms can have healing properties, and the intention and energy infused into the charm can help amplify these properties.

When creating a mojo bag or gris-gris for healing purposes, it is important to set the intention for the charm and focus on the desired outcome. The materials used in the charm should be chosen based on their healing properties, and the charm should be infused with positive energy and intention. The charm can then be carried or worn to promote healing and protection. It is important to note that while mojo bags and gris-gris can be powerful tools for promoting healing, they should not replace medical treatment. It is always important to seek medical advice and treatment when dealing with health issues. Mojo bags and gris-gris can be used alongside medical treatment to promote healing and well-being.

Prosperity and abundance: In Voodoo, prosperity and abundance are considered important aspects of a well-lived life. While financial wealth is not the only measure of prosperity, it is certainly an important aspect of it. Voodoo charms can attract wealth, success, and abundance in all areas of life. The use of mojo bags and gris-gris in Voodoo is often linked to harnessing the universe's power to achieve one's goals. It is believed that by creating a physical representation of one's desires, such as a mojo bag or gris-gris, and imbuing it with spiritual power, you can draw the desired outcome into your life.

For those seeking prosperity and abundance, Voodoo charms can attract wealth and success and increase opportunities for financial gain. These charms may include symbolic items such as coins or dollar bills, herbs, and other natural materials believed to have magical properties. It is important to note that Voodoo does not teach that wealth and prosperity are the only measures of success or happiness. Rather, true prosperity is believed to encompass all aspects of life, including emotional, spiritual, and social well-being. Therefore, Voodoo charms used for prosperity and abundance may also include personal growth and fulfillment items, such as crystals or symbols of personal goals.

Overall, Voodoo charms used for prosperity and abundance are intended to help individuals align their energy with the universe, increasing the likelihood of success in all areas of life. While financial gain is often a desired outcome, true prosperity also involves emotional and spiritual fulfillment, making Voodoo a holistic approach to achieving prosperity and abundance.

Legal matters: Mojo bags and gris-gris are not just used for spiritual purposes but can also be used to aid in legal matters. These charms can help with success in court cases or negotiations, as well as giving protection from legal harm. The power of these charms lies in their ability to connect the individual to the spiritual realm and provide guidance and protection. Voodoo practitioners believe that by creating a mojo bag or gris-gris, they are tapping into the power of their ancestors and spirits to guide them in their legal matters.

These charms can be carried on your body or placed strategically to provide maximum benefit. When used in legal matters, the mojo bag or gris-gris can help to provide a clear mind and a strong presence, making it easier to present a strong case or negotiate favorable terms. In addition, the mojo bag or gris-gris can protect from negative energy, including those directed toward the individual in legal proceedings. This can help ensure the individual is not wrongfully accused or unfairly punished.

Spiritual connection: Voodoo charms attract material blessings or protection from negative energies and can also enhance your spiritual connections. The practice of Voodoo involves a belief in the existence of a spirit world that is interconnected with the physical world. Because of this, Voodoo charms can be used to enhance spiritual connections with the divine, ancestors, and spirits. One way voodoo charms can help with spiritual connection is by physically representing your intentions and prayers. When you create a mojo bag or gris-gris, you physically manifest your desires and needs. By carrying or wearing the charm, you remind yourself of your spiritual goals and the energy you put into achieving them.

In addition, voodoo charms can be used in rituals or ceremonies to enhance spiritual connections. For example, a mojo bag may be used in a ritual to connect with ancestors or ask spirits for guidance. The presence of the charm can serve as a focal point for your intentions and prayers, allowing you to deepen your spiritual connections. Furthermore, the materials used to create voodoo charms can also have spiritual significance. For example, certain herbs or crystals are believed to have spiritual properties that can enhance spiritual connections or help in spiritual healing. By including these materials in a mojo bag or gris-gris, you are utilizing their spiritual properties to enhance your own spiritual connections.

Tips and Tricks to Adapt Charms to Your Needs

1. **Personalize the ingredients:** While traditional ingredients are often used in mojo bags and gris-gris, choosing ingredients that resonate with you and your intentions is important. Consider using herbs or other materials with personal significance or specific properties that align with your desired outcome.

2. **Customize the color:** The color of the fabric used to make a mojo bag or gris-gris can also be personalized to fit your intentions. Consider choosing a color corresponding to the specific purpose of your charm, such as green for money or red for love.

3. **Incorporate personal items:** Adding personal items to your mojo bag or gris-gris can help strengthen your connection to the charm and your intentions. This could include a piece of jewelry, a small photo, or a written intention.

4. **Charge and activate the charm:** Before using your charm, take the time to charge it with your intentions and activate its energy. This can be done through prayer, meditation, or other ritual practices. *Remember that breathing on the charm is vital.*

5. **Recharge the charm as needed:** As you continue to use your mojo bag or gris-gris, it may lose some of its energy over time. Consider recharging it periodically with intention-setting and energy-activating practices to keep it effective.

Chapter Nine: Cleansing and Raising Protections

While the popular media often portrays Voodoo and Hoodoo as being all about curses and hexes, the truth is that the best offense is a good defense. It's essential to remember that Voodoo and Hoodoo are primarily spiritual practices that focus on protection, healing, and helping people achieve their goals. One of the most effective ways to protect yourself is by taking a spiritual bath. This practice involves using a combination of herbs, oils, and other ingredients to cleanse yourself spiritually and protect yourself from negative energies. When done correctly, a spiritual bath can help you feel more balanced, centered, and grounded, as well as help you release any negative energy you may be carrying around.

In addition to spiritual baths, there are various rituals and spells you can use to protect yourself from negative energies and influences. These could include creating a protective charm or talisman, performing a ritual to banish negative energy, or casting a spell to protect yourself from harm. Another important aspect of protection in Voodoo and Hoodoo is working with spiritual allies. This could include calling on your ancestors or other spirits for protection and guidance or creating a relationship with a particular deity or spirit who is known for providing protection and support.

There are a number of rituals and spells available that provide protection.

One of the most important things to remember when working with protection in Voodoo and Hoodoo is that it's not just about defending yourself from outside influences. It's also about cultivating a strong, positive energy within yourself that can help you stay centered and focused no matter your challenges. To that end, it's important to cultivate a regular spiritual practice that includes prayer, meditation, and other practices that help you connect with your inner self and the divine. This could involve creating a daily ritual that includes lighting candles, burning incense, and reciting prayers or mantras. It might also involve working with a particular spiritual teacher or guide who can help you deepen your spiritual practice.

Legba's Shield Bath (For Self-Protection)

Materials:

- Eucalyptus leaves
- Lemongrass
- Bay leaves
- Mint leaves
- 7 white candles
- A white cloth
- Florida water (*a sort of citrus cologne*)
- Protection oil
- A photo of yourself
- A bowl

Steps:

1. Begin by lighting the candles and placing them in a circle around you.
2. Add the eucalyptus leaves, lemongrass, bay leaves, and mint leaves to a bowl of hot water.
3. Place the bowl on the white cloth in front of you.
4. Add a few drops of Florida water and protection oil to the bowl.
5. Hold the photo of yourself in your hands and focus on your intention of protection.
6. Call upon your ancestors and ask them to bless your bath.
7. Call upon the Lwa of protection, Papa Legba, and ask for his assistance.
8. Add the photo to the bowl and stir the water with your hand.
9. Recite a protection prayer or affirmation.
10. Stand in the middle of the candle circle and pour the bathwater over your head while reciting a prayer for protection.
11. Once you have poured all the water over your head, extinguish the candles.

Fiery Shield Spell (For Self-Protection)

Materials:

- A red candle
- Dragon's Blood oil
- A photo of yourself
- A piece of red cloth
- Protection powder
- A small mirror
- A piece of black string
- A bowl

Steps:

1. Anoint the red candle with Dragon's Blood oil and place it in the center of the bowl.
2. Light the candle and focus on your desire to be safe and protected.
3. Focus on your ancestors, calling on them to bear witness to and bless this ritual.
4. Hold the photo of yourself in your hands and recite an invocation to the Lwa of protection, Papa Legba.
5. Rub the protection powder onto the red cloth and wrap it around the small mirror.
6. Tie the piece of black string around the bundle.
7. Hold the bundle in front of the lit candle and recite a prayer or affirmation for protection.
8. Place the bundle next to the candle and let the candle burn down completely.
9. Keep the bundle with you at all times for protection.

Ironclad Shield Spell (For the Protection of Someone Else)

Materials:

- A black candle
- Protection oil
- A photo of the person you wish to protect
- A piece of iron or steel
- A black cloth
- Black thread
- A bowl

Steps:

1. Anoint the black candle with protection oil and place it in the center of the bowl.
2. Light the candle and focus on your intention of protection.
3. Call upon your ancestors so they can bless and witness your ritual.
4. In your hands, hold the photo of the person you wish to protect and recite an invocation to the Lwa of protection, Ogun.
5. Place the photo in the bowl and lay the piece of iron or steel on top of it.
6. Wrap the black cloth around the bowl and tie it with the black thread.
7. Let the candle burn down completely.
8. Remove the cloth bundle from the bowl and bury it in the earth, preferably near the person you wish to protect.

Saved by Danto Spell (For Home Protection)

Materials:

- A white candle
- Protection herbs (such as bay leaves, thyme, and rosemary)
- A small bowl of salt
- A black cloth
- A piece of red string
- A photo of your home
- A bowl

Steps:

1. Light the white candle and place it in the center of the bowl.
2. Sprinkle the protection herbs around the candle.
3. Call upon your ancestors to bless your ritual.
4. Hold the photo of your home in your hands and recite an invocation to the Lwa of protection, Ezili Danto.
5. Place the photo in the bowl and sprinkle the small bowl of salt over it.
6. Wrap the black cloth around the bowl and tie it with the red string.
7. Let the candle burn down completely.
8. Remove the cloth bundle from the bowl and place it in a prominent location in your home for continued protection.

Divine Guardian Charm (To Protect Yourself or Someone Else)

Materials:

- A small white cloth
- White thread
- Protection oil
- A photo of the person you wish to protect
- Dried bay leaves
- A small white feather
- A small clear quartz crystal

Steps:

1. Begin by cutting the white cloth into a circular shape.
2. Place the photo of the person you wish to protect in the center of the cloth.
3. Call your ancestors to bless your work.
4. Add a few drops of protection oil on top of the photo.
5. Sprinkle some dried bay leaves around the photo.
6. Place the small white feather on top of the bay leaves.
7. Place the clear quartz crystal on top of the feather.
8. Gather the edges of the cloth together and tie it with the white thread.
9. Hold the charm in your hands and call upon Baron Samedi, asking for his assistance in protecting the person.
10. Invoke the person's ancestors and ask for their protection and guidance.
11. Give the charm to the person to carry with them at all times.

Sanctuary Charm (For Protecting the Home)

Materials:

- A small black cloth
- Black thread
- Protection oil
- A small jar with a lid
- Dried sage
- Dried rosemary
- A piece of black tourmaline
- Black salt

Steps:

1. Begin by cutting the black cloth into a square shape.
2. Place the dried sage and rosemary in the jar.
3. Add a few drops of protection oil on top of the herbs.
4. Place the black tourmaline in the jar.
5. Sprinkle some black salt on top of the tourmaline.
6. Close the lid of the jar tightly.
7. Wrap the jar with the black cloth and tie it with the black thread.
8. Hold the charm in your hands and call upon the Lwa of protection, Ogun, asking for his assistance in protecting the home.
9. Invoke your ancestors and ask for their protection and guidance as well.
10. Place the charm in a location within the home where it can be seen, such as on a shelf or mantelpiece.

Note that you can call on any Lwa you want whom you would prefer to protect you and that you can always substitute one material for another. You will need to refer to the glossary at the end of the book to learn what works for what.

Have You Been Hexed?

It is not uncommon for individuals who practice Voodoo to experience hexes or curses from other practitioners. A hex can cause harm and misfortune in many areas of your life, from health to career and relationships. If you suspect you have been hexed, taking immediate steps to protect yourself and reverse the curse's effects is important.

Following are several tips to help you check whether you have been hexed by another Voodoo practitioner or not, and they explain how to purge the hex and protect yourself in the future:

1. Pay attention to sudden changes in your life. If you have been experiencing a sudden string of bad luck or misfortune, it could be a sign that you have been hexed. Common signs of a hex include financial, relationship, health, and career setbacks.

2. Look for physical symptoms. A hex can also cause physical symptoms such as headaches, fatigue, and digestive issues. If you are experiencing unexplained physical symptoms, it could be a sign that you have been hexed.

3. Consult with a trusted Voodoo practitioner. If you suspect you have been hexed, seeking help from a trusted Voodoo practitioner is important. They can help you determine whether you have been hexed and guide you on reversing the curse's effects.

4. Perform a cleansing ritual. You can perform a cleansing ritual to purge the hex and cleanse yourself of negative energy. This can involve taking a bath with herbs and oils, smudging your home with sage or palo santo, or burning candles to symbolize the release of negative energy.

5. Invoke the help of a powerful Lwa. To protect yourself from future hexes, you can invoke the help of a powerful Lwa, such as Papa Legba, who is known for his ability to protect against evil and negative energy. You can offer him tobacco, rum, or coffee offerings and ask for his protection.

6. Wear protective amulets. To protect yourself from future hexes, you can wear protective amulets such as a mojo bag or a talisman made with materials such as herbs, crystals, and oils. Once made, the bag or talisman can be carried with you at all times.

7. Avoid negative people and situations. Avoiding negative people and situations that could attract negative energy is important to prevent future hexes. Surround yourself with positive people and focus on positive thoughts and actions.

8. Practice Daily Protection Rituals: Once you have had a hex removed, protecting yourself from future attacks is important. Practice daily protection rituals, such as lighting candles or carrying protective talismans. You can also create a protective mojo bag to carry with you always. Incorporate protective herbs, such as bay leaves or sage, into your home and personal space. By taking these steps, you can create a shield of protection around yourself and ward off any future attacks.

Chapter Ten: Voodoo for Love and Abundance

In the previous chapter, you learned how to perform spells, baths, rituals, and charms for protection. Now, it's time to address matters of the heart — and the pocket. The Voodooist knows they have the power to manifest these desires into their lives by creating charms. As a Voodooist, you understand that charms and spells are based on the power of intention, the beauty of creation, and the magic of the divine. So, you'll master the art of making charms, baths, and spells to open the floodgates of love and abundance in your life.

Passion Bath (For Drawing Love to You)

Materials:

- Red rose petals
- Patchouli essential oil
- Cinnamon sticks or cinnamon essential oil
- A red cloth
- A photo or personal item of the person you wish to attract
- 7 red candles
- A bowl

Steps:

1. Begin by lighting the candles and placing them in a circle around the bowl.

2. Add the red rose petals, a few drops of patchouli essential oil, and a cinnamon stick or a few drops of cinnamon essential oil to the bowl of hot water.

3. Place the bowl on the red cloth in front of you.

4. Hold the photo or personal item of the person you wish to attract in your hands and focus on your intention of attracting their love.

5. Call upon the Lwa of love and passion, Ezili Freda, and ask for her help to bring the person's love into your life.

6. Invoke your ancestors and ask for their guidance and protection.

7. Once you feel that the photo or personal item has been charged, remove it from the bowl and dry it off.

8. Step into the bath and soak for at least 20 minutes while meditating on your intention and positive affirmations.

9. Pour the remaining bathwater over the candles to extinguish them.

Self-Love Fountain Spell

Materials:

- A red or pink candle
- Rose petals
- Lavender oil
- Honey
- A small mirror
- Red or pink fabric
- Red or pink ribbon
- A piece of paper and a pen

Steps:

1. Begin by lighting the candle and placing it in front of you.
2. Write down affirmations of self-love on the piece of paper, such as "I love and accept myself just as I am" or "I radiate love and confidence."
3. Hold the mirror up to your face and recite the affirmations aloud.
4. Dip your finger in the honey and anoint the candle with it, saying, *"I am sweet, deserving, and loved."*
5. Sprinkle rose petals around the candle and drizzle a few drops of lavender oil over them.
6. Fold the paper with your affirmations and place it under the candle.
7. Wrap the candle, paper, and petals in the red or pink fabric and tie it closed with the ribbon.
8. Hold the charm to your heart and say, *"I am worthy of love, and I love myself."*
9. Ask the Lwa of love, Erzulie Freda, for her blessings and assistance in your self-love journey.
10. Keep the charm on your person or in a safe place as a reminder of your self-love intentions.

Love Drawing Spell

Materials:

- Red or pink love mojo bag
- Rose petals
- Cinnamon sticks
- Catnip
- Ginger root
- Lodestone
- A piece of paper and a pen

Steps:

1. Begin by writing down the qualities you desire in a partner on a piece of paper.
2. Fill the mojo bag with rose petals, cinnamon sticks, catnip, and ginger root.
3. Place the lodestone in the center of the herbs.
4. Fold the paper with your desired qualities and place it in the mojo bag.
5. Hold the mojo bag in your hands and recite, *"I attract the love that is true, pure, and good for me."*
6. Ask the Lwa of love and attraction, Erzili Dantor, for her assistance in manifesting your desires.
7. Keep the mojo bag on your person or in a safe place, focusing on your intentions for love and keeping an open heart.

Loving Home Spell

Materials:

- Pink or red candles (one for each member of the household)
- Vanilla oil
- Honey
- A bowl of salt
- A piece of paper and a pen

Steps:

1. Begin by lighting a pink or red candle for each household member.
2. Write down each member's name on the piece of paper and place it in the bowl of salt.
3. Anoint each candle with a drop of vanilla oil and a drizzle of honey, saying, *"May love and harmony fill our home."*
4. Light each candle and sprinkle a pinch of salt over the flame, saying, *"May negativity and discord be banished from our home."*
5. Hold hands with your family members as the candles burn and recite a prayer or affirmation for love and unity.
6. Ask the Lwa you've chosen for their blessings and protection over your household.
7. Allow the candles to burn down completely or snuff them out with a snuffer, but never blow them out.
8. Dispose of the salt and paper by burying them outside of your home.

Note: It is important to perform this spell with the consent and participation of all household members.

Golden Opportunity Charm

Materials:

- A small golden coin or charm
- A green or gold drawstring bag
- Cinnamon sticks
- Bay leaves
- Cloves
- Allspice berries

Steps:

1. Begin by invoking the Lwa of prosperity, Ayizan, and calling on your ancestors for their guidance and blessings.
2. Hold the golden coin or charm in your hands and visualize yourself receiving abundance and financial opportunities.
3. Place the coin or charm into the green or gold drawstring bag.
4. Add in the cinnamon sticks, bay leaves, cloves, and allspice berries.
5. Close the bag and shake it gently, saying, *"Opportunities come my way; prosperity is here to stay."*
6. Carry the charm with you, or keep it in a safe place in your home or office.

Wealthy Path Charm

Materials:

- A small green cloth or sachet
- A dollar bill or other currency
- Peppermint leaves
- Alfalfa
- Pyrite crystal
- A small gold-colored charm or trinket

Steps:

1. Begin by invoking Damballa and calling on your ancestors for guidance and blessings.
2. Place the dollar bill or currency in the center of the green cloth or sachet.
3. Add in the peppermint leaves and alfalfa.
4. Place the pyrite crystal on top of the dollar bill or currency.
5. Add the small gold-colored charm or trinket.
6. Tie up the cloth or sachet with a gold ribbon or string, saying, *"Wealth and prosperity come my way, blessings for me every day."*
7. Keep the charm with you, or place it in a prominent location in your home or office.

Success and Prosperity Charm

Materials:

- A small red or gold bag
- Three cinnamon sticks
- Allspice berries
- Bay leaves
- A small piece of citrine crystal

Steps:

1. Begin by invoking the Lwa of opportunity, Papa Legba, and calling on your ancestors for their guidance and blessings.
2. Place the cinnamon sticks, allspice berries, and bay leaves into the red or gold bag.
3. Add the citrine crystal to the bag.
4. Hold the bag in your hands and visualize yourself achieving success and prosperity in your business or career.
5. Tie up the bag with a red or gold ribbon or string, saying, *"Success and prosperity come my way; blessings for me every day."*
6. Keep the charm with you, or place it in a prominent location in your office or workspace.

Gold Fortune Bath

Materials:

- Bay leaves
- Cinnamon sticks
- Dried chamomile flowers
- Gold glitter
- Honey
- Coconut milk
- Yellow candle
- Bathtub

Steps:

1. Light the yellow candle and place it near the bathtub.
2. Add a handful of bay leaves, a few cinnamon sticks, and a small amount of dried chamomile flowers to the bathwater.
3. Add a pinch of gold glitter and a tablespoon of honey to the bathwater.
4. Pour in a can of coconut milk and mix everything together.
5. Soak in the bath, visualizing yourself surrounded by golden light and abundance.
6. Invoke the Lwa of prosperity, Erzili Freda, by saying, *"Erzili Freda, please bless me with your love and abundance."*
7. Invoke your ancestors by saying, *"Ancestors, please guide and protect me on my path to prosperity."*

Fortunate Business Bath

Materials:

- Green tea bags
- Dried basil leaves
- Dried rosemary
- Green glitter
- Patchouli oil
- Green candle
- Bathtub

Steps:

1. Light the green candle and place it near the bathtub.
2. Add 2-3 green tea bags, a handful of dried basil leaves, and a few dried rosemary sprigs to the bathwater.
3. Add a pinch of green glitter and a few drops of patchouli oil to the bathwater.
4. Soak in the bath, visualizing success and abundance in your business or career.
5. Invoke Papa Legba by saying, *"Papa Legba, please open the gates to success and prosperity in my business/career."*
6. Invoke your ancestors by saying, *"Ancestors, please guide and protect me on my path to financial success."*

Be Prosperous Bath

Materials:

- Dried lavender
- Dried chamomile flowers
- Honey
- White candle
- Bathtub

Steps:

1. Light the white candle and place it near the bathtub.
2. Add a handful of dried lavender and a small amount of dried chamomile flowers to the bathwater.
3. Add a tablespoon of honey to the bathwater.
4. Soak in the bath, visualizing abundance and prosperity for the person you wish to help.
5. Invoke Loko by saying, *"Loko, please bless (person's name) with abundance and prosperity."*
6. Invoke your ancestors by saying, *"Ancestors, please guide and protect (person's name) on their path to prosperity."*

Crafting Your Own Rituals

Voodoo rituals are a powerful and sacred practice that requires careful preparation and execution. To create a successful and effective ritual, it's important to understand the general structure that most Voodoo rituals follow. Voodoo rituals are usually divided into four stages:

- Preparation
- Invocation
- Possession
- Farewell

The first stage, preparation, is crucial to the ritual's success. During this stage, the practitioner will gather all of the materials they need for the ritual, including herbs, candles, and other tools. They will also prepare the physical space where the ritual will take place. This may involve setting up an altar or other sacred space and cleansing and purifying the area to remove any negative energy or entities.

In the second stage, invocation, the practitioner calls upon the spirits and deities to aid them in their work. This is typically done through prayers, invocations, and offerings, such as food or drink. During this stage, the practitioner may also make requests or petitions to the spirits or deities for specific outcomes or blessings.

In the third stage, possession, the practitioner may enter a trance state and become possessed by the spirits or deities. This can be a powerful and transformative experience, allowing the practitioner to gain insights and receive guidance from the spirits. During possession, the practitioner may speak in tongues, dance, or physically express the spirits' presence. In your personal rituals, this can simply be you feeling the energy of the Lwa in and around you.

In the final stage, the practitioner bids farewell to the spirits and deities and releases them from the physical space. This may involve offering thanks and gratitude for their assistance and cleansing and purifying the area again to remove any lingering energy or entities. It's important to note that not all Voodoo rituals will follow this exact structure, and different practitioners may have their own variations and methods. However, understanding the general structure can provide a helpful framework for creating your own rituals or participating in those led by others.

Cloves - provide protection, healing, and love. This is used in protection and love spells.

Comfrey Root - brings safety, protection, and healing. This is used in spells for safety and protection.

Dragon's Blood - enhances power and success. This is used in spells for protection and empowerment.

Eucalyptus - brings healing and purification; used in healing and cleansing spells.

Fennel - enhances psychic abilities and brings protection. This is used in divination and protection spells.

Frankincense - provides protection, purification, and spiritual growth. This is used in purification and protection spells.

Galangal Root - brings good luck, love, and protection and is used in love and protection spells.

Ginger - enhances power and success and is used in spells for success and good fortune.

Hawthorn Berry - provides protection, purification, and good luck and is used in protection and healing spells.

Hyssop - brings purification and protection and is used in purification and protection spells.

Jasmine - enhances psychic abilities and love and can be used in love and divination spells.

Juniper Berries - brings purification and protection and can be used in purification and protection spells.

Lavender - brings calmness, love, and purification and is used in love and purification spells.

Lemon Balm - brings love and success and is used in love and success spells.

Lemongrass - brings purification, love, and healing and is used in purification and love spells.

Licorice Root - enhances power and success and is often used in spells for success and good fortune.

Mandrake Root - enhances power and protection and is used in spells for protection and empowerment.

Mint - brings prosperity, healing, and protection and is used in money and healing spells.

Crafting Your Own Rituals

Voodoo rituals are a powerful and sacred practice that requires careful preparation and execution. To create a successful and effective ritual, it's important to understand the general structure that most Voodoo rituals follow. Voodoo rituals are usually divided into four stages:

- Preparation
- Invocation
- Possession
- Farewell

The first stage, preparation, is crucial to the ritual's success. During this stage, the practitioner will gather all of the materials they need for the ritual, including herbs, candles, and other tools. They will also prepare the physical space where the ritual will take place. This may involve setting up an altar or other sacred space and cleansing and purifying the area to remove any negative energy or entities.

In the second stage, invocation, the practitioner calls upon the spirits and deities to aid them in their work. This is typically done through prayers, invocations, and offerings, such as food or drink. During this stage, the practitioner may also make requests or petitions to the spirits or deities for specific outcomes or blessings.

In the third stage, possession, the practitioner may enter a trance state and become possessed by the spirits or deities. This can be a powerful and transformative experience, allowing the practitioner to gain insights and receive guidance from the spirits. During possession, the practitioner may speak in tongues, dance, or physically express the spirits' presence. In your personal rituals, this can simply be you feeling the energy of the Lwa in and around you.

In the final stage, the practitioner bids farewell to the spirits and deities and releases them from the physical space. This may involve offering thanks and gratitude for their assistance and cleansing and purifying the area again to remove any lingering energy or entities. It's important to note that not all Voodoo rituals will follow this exact structure, and different practitioners may have their own variations and methods. However, understanding the general structure can provide a helpful framework for creating your own rituals or participating in those led by others.

In addition to the four stages, it's also important to consider the intention and energy behind the ritual. The practitioner should approach the ritual with a clear and focused intention and strongly believe in the power of the spirits and deities to assist them in their work. They should also be respectful and mindful of the spirits and deities, offering gratitude and honor for their assistance.

Mugwort - enhances psychic abilities and brings protection and is often used in divination and protection spells.

Myrrh - provides purification, protection, and spiritual growth and is used in purification and protection spells.

Nettle - brings protection, healing, and purification and is used in protection and healing spells.

Orange Peel - enhances love and brings good luck and is used in love and luck spells.

Patchouli - enhances love, prosperity, and protection and is used in love and money spells.

Peppermint - brings prosperity, healing, and protection and is used in money and healing spells.

Pine - brings purification, protection, and healing and can be used in purification and healing spells.

Red Pepper - brings protection and good luck and is often used in protection and money spells.

Rose - enhances love and brings healing and is commonly used in love and healing spells.

Rosemary - brings purification, protection, and love and is used in purification and love spells.

Sandalwood - enhances spirituality, brings calmness and clarity, and is used in meditation and purification spells.

Sarsaparilla Root - provides protection and enhances sexual potency and is often used in protection and love spells.

Solomon's Seal Root - brings protection and healing and can be used in protection and healing spells.

St. John's Wort - brings happiness, protection, and purification. This can be used in protection and purification spells.

Thyme - brings purification, courage, and psychic abilities. It is used in purification and courage spells.

Valerian Root - enhances love, brings calmness and sleep, and can be used in love and sleep spells.

Vervain - enhances spirituality, brings protection and purification, and is used in purification and protection spells.

Vetiver - enhances love and brings grounding and protection – often used in love and protection spells.

White Sage - brings purification and protection and can be used in purification and protection spells.

Wormwood - enhances psychic abilities and brings protection and can be used in divination and protection spells.

Yarrow - brings courage, protection, and love – often used in courage and love spells.

Yerba Santa - brings purification, healing, and protection and is used in purification and healing spells.

Yucca Root - enhances spiritual power, brings protection and prosperity, it is used in protection and money spells.

Note: In Voodoo, herbs and roots play a significant role in the practice of magic, as they are believed to possess spiritual properties that can aid in spells and rituals. The herbs and roots listed above have different spiritual meanings, roles, and uses in spells. Some are used for protection, purification, and healing, while others are used for love, prosperity, and success. When using herbs and roots in spells, it is essential to understand their properties and how they can be incorporated into the spell. Some herbs may be burned, brewed in tea, carried in a sachet, or used in a bath. The choice of which herb or root you use may also depend on the goal of the spell and be relevant to the specific Lwa or ancestor being invoked. It is important to note that while herbs and roots can be potent aids in spells and rituals, they are not a replacement for professional medical or legal advice. Voodoo is a powerful and complex spiritual practice, and it should be approached with respect, understanding, and caution.

Oils

African Musk Oil - brings protection, love, and prosperity and is used in love and money spells.

Allspice Oil - enhances power and success and can be used in spells for success and good fortune.

Amber Oil - provides protection and attracts love. Thus, it is used in protection and love spells.

Anise Oil - brings purification, psychic abilities, and protection. This is used in divination and protection spells.

Basil Oil - attracts prosperity, love, and peace. Often it is used in love and money spells.

Bayberry Oil - brings prosperity and abundance. It is used in money and prosperity spells.

Benzoin Oil - provides purification, protection, and spiritual growth. This is used in purification and protection spells.

Black Pepper Oil - brings protection, purification, and success. It is used in protection and success spells.

Calamus Oil - brings good luck, money, and healing and is used in spells for success and good fortune.

Camphor Oil - repels negativity and evil; and is used in purification and protection spells.

Cardamom Oil - enhances love and brings good luck and is used in love and luck spells.

Cedarwood Oil - brings purification, protection, and healing and can be used in purification and healing spells.

Chamomile Oil - brings love and purification and is used in love and purification spells.

Cinnamon Oil - brings success, prosperity, and love and is used in money and love spells.

Citronella Oil - repels negativity and evil and can be used in purification and protection spells.

Clove Oil - provides protection, healing, and love and is often used in protection and love spells.

Coconut Oil - brings purification, protection, and success and is used in purification and success spells.

Eucalyptus Oil - brings healing and purification and is thus used in healing and cleansing spells.

Frankincense Oil - provides protection, purification, and spiritual growth and is used in purification and protection spells.

Gardenia Oil - enhances love and brings success, often used in love and success spells.

Ginger Oil - enhances power and success and is used in spells for success and good fortune.

Grapefruit Oil - brings purification and healing and is thus used in purification and healing spells.

Jasmine Oil - enhances psychic abilities and love and can be used in love and divination spells.

Lavender Oil - brings calmness, love, and purification and is sometimes used in love and purification spells.

Lemongrass Oil - brings purification, love, and healing and is used in purification and love spells.

Lime Oil - brings purification and protection and is used in purification and protection spells.

Lotus Oil - enhances spiritual growth and brings love and is used in spiritual and love spells.

Magnolia Oil - enhances love and brings good luck and is used in love and luck spells.

Myrrh Oil - provides purification, protection, and spiritual growth and can be used in purification and protection spells

Neroli Oil - enhances love and brings purification. It is used in love and purification spells.

Orange Oil - brings purification and enhances love. It is used in purification and love spells.

Patchouli Oil - enhances love, prosperity, and protection and is often used in love and money spells.

Peppermint Oil - brings prosperity, healing, and protection. It is used in money and healing spells.

Pine Oil - brings purification, protection, and healing. It is used in purification and healing spells.

Rose Oil - enhances love and brings healing and is used in love and healing spells.

Rosemary Oil - brings purification, protection, and love and is often used in purification and love spells.

Rue Oil - provides protection, purification, and healing and is used in protection and purification spells.

Sandalwood Oil - enhances spiritual growth, protection, and healing and is used in spiritual and healing spells.

Spearmint Oil - brings healing and purification and can be used in healing and purification spells.

Sweetgrass Oil - enhances spiritual growth and brings purification and is used in spiritual and purification spells.

Tangerine Oil - enhances love and brings purification and is therefore used in love and purification spells.

Tea Tree Oil - brings healing and protection and is used in healing and protection spells.

Thyme Oil - enhances psychic abilities and brings purification and is used in divination and purification spells.

Vanilla Oil - enhances love and brings good luck and is used in love and luck spells.

Vetiver Oil - enhances protection, purification, and grounding. This is used in protection and purification spells.

Wisteria Oil - enhances psychic abilities and brings success. This is used in divination and success spells.

Yarrow Oil - enhances psychic abilities and brings love. It is often used in divination and love spells.

Ylang Ylang Oil - enhances love and brings purification. It is used in love and purification spells.

Zedoary Oil - brings purification and enhances psychic abilities. This is used in purification and divination spells.

Please note that these oils and their corresponding spiritual meanings, roles, and usages may vary depending on the practitioner and tradition of Voodoo. It is important to always research and consult with a trusted and experienced practitioner before using any oils or conducting any spells.

Candles

Candles are an important tool in Voodoo rituals and spells. They are often used to focus the practitioner's intention and provide a physical representation of the energy directed towards a particular goal or outcome. The candle color used in a spell can play an important role in its effectiveness, as each color is associated with a particular intention or energy. Here are some common candle colors used in Voodoo, along with their meanings and spiritual uses:

White: purity, clarity, healing, and protection. White candles can be used for any purpose, as they represent the purest and most neutral form of energy.

Black: banishing, protecting, and breaking curses. Black candles are often used in spells to remove negative energy or protect against harm.

Red: love, passion, strength, and courage. Red candles can be used in spells related to romantic love, as well as to boost personal power and confidence.

Pink: love, friendship, and emotional healing. Pink candles are often used in spells related to emotional healing, self-love, and friendship.

Blue: calmness, communication, and healing. Blue candles can be used in spells related to clear communication, peacefulness, and emotional healing.

Green: abundance, prosperity, and growth. Green candles can be used in spells related to money, success, and personal growth.

Yellow: clarity, intellect, and creativity. Yellow candles can be used in spells related to mental clarity, focus, and creativity.

Purple: spiritual power, intuition, and psychic abilities. Purple candles can be used in spells related to spiritual growth, psychic abilities, and intuition.

Orange: energy, enthusiasm, and success. Orange candles can be used in spells related to success, enthusiasm, and increased energy.

In addition to the different colors, there are also different types of candles used in Voodoo. Some practitioners prefer to use beeswax candles, as they are considered to be more natural and powerful than other types of candles. Some also prefer to use tapered candles, which can be carved with symbols or inscriptions related to the intended outcome of the spell.

Disclaimer: Whatever you do, please do not ingest any oils or herbs, as they can be dangerous. When applying oil to the skin, please do a patch test first by applying a small amount on the inner part of your wrist and then wait a day to see if you have any adverse reaction. Please note that you should keep your herbs, roots, and oils away from children and pets so they don't hurt themselves. Store them safely away where only you can reach them.

Conclusion

You have reached the end of "Voodoo for Beginners - A guide to New Orleans Voodoo, Haitian Vodou, and Hoodoo." Thank you for taking the time to read this book and explore Voodoo's rich and fascinating world. Throughout this book, you have gained an understanding of Voodoo's history, beliefs, practices, and traditions. You have learned about the differences between New Orleans Voodoo, Haitian Vodou, and Hoodoo and how each of these practices can be used to help you achieve your desires and goals.

You have discovered the importance of connecting with ancestors and spirits and how to work with them to manifest positive change in your life. Remember, the core principles of Voodoo are faith, respect, and gratitude. When you approach this practice with an open mind and heart and with the intention to help yourself and others, you will be rewarded with powerful spiritual experiences and meaningful connections.

As you begin to incorporate the practices and rituals of Voodoo into your daily life, remember that consistency and dedication are key. The more you practice, the stronger your connection with the spirits and ancestors will become, and the more effective your spells and rituals will be. It is also important to continue your studies and seek out guidance from those who have practiced longer than you have. Attend local Voodoo ceremonies and events, and connect with others who share your interest in this spiritual practice. There is always more to learn; by seeking new knowledge and experiences, you will continue to grow and evolve in your practice.

Finally, remember that Voodoo is a powerful tool for personal growth and transformation, but it is not a substitute for professional help. Suppose you are experiencing serious physical, emotional, or mental health issues. In that case, it is important to seek the advice and guidance of a qualified medical or mental health professional. In closing, may you continue to explore this fascinating and powerful spiritual practice with an open mind and heart, and may the spirits and ancestors guide and bless you on your path.

Here's another book by Mari Silva that you might like

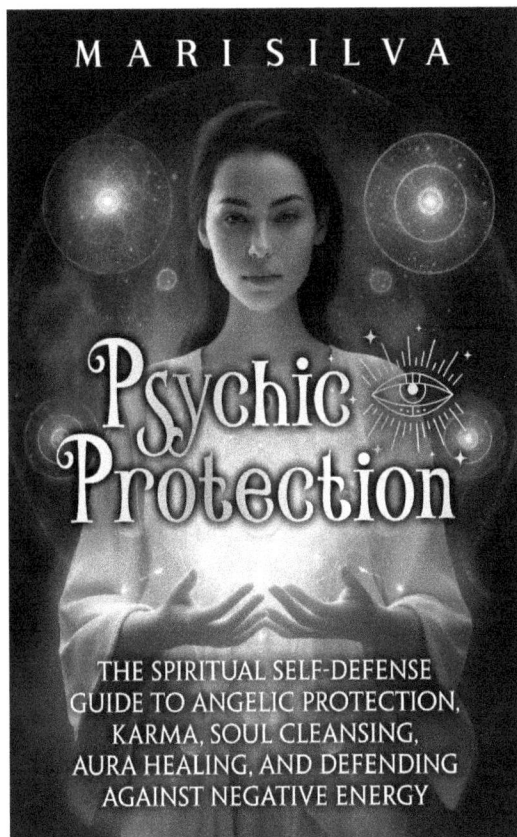

MARI SILVA

Psychic Protection

THE SPIRITUAL SELF-DEFENSE
GUIDE TO ANGELIC PROTECTION,
KARMA, SOUL CLEANSING,
AURA HEALING, AND DEFENDING
AGAINST NEGATIVE ENERGY

Your Free Gift
(only available for a limited time)

Thanks for getting this book! If you want to learn more about various spirituality topics, then join Mari Silva's community and get a free guided meditation MP3 for awakening your third eye. This guided meditation mp3 is designed to open and strengthen ones third eye so you can experience a higher state of consciousness. Simply visit the link below the image to get started.

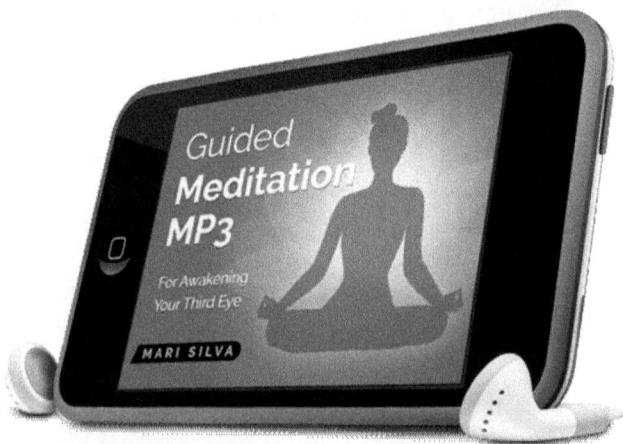

https://spiritualityspot.com/meditation

References

Desmangles, L. (1992). The Faces of the Gods: Vodou and Roman Catholicism in Haiti. University of North Carolina Press.

Fandrich, I. J. (2005). The Birth of New Orleans' Voodoo Queen: A Long-Held Mystery Resolved. Louisiana History

Fandrich, I. J. (2007). Yorùbá influences Haitian vodou and New Orleans voodoo. Journal of Black Studies.

Filan, K. (2010). The Haitian Vodou Handbook: Protocols for Riding with the Lwa. Destiny Books.

Guenin-Lelle, D. (2016). The Story of French New Orleans: History of a Creole City. Univ. Press of Mississippi.

Hazzard-Donald, K. (2012). Mojo workin': The old African American hoodoo system. University of Illinois Press.

Hebblethwaite, B. (2012). Vodou Songs in Haitian Creole and English. Temple University Press.

Hurston, Z. (1931). Hoodoo in America. The Journal of American Folklore.

McAlister, E. (2002). Rara! Vodou, Power, and Performance in Haiti and its Diaspora. University of California Press.

Murphy, J. (2011). Working the Spirit: Ceremonies of the African Diaspora. Beacon Press.

Packham, J. (2012). Voodoo. The Encyclopedia of the Gothic.

Stewart, L. (2017). Work the Root: Black Feminism, Hoodoo Love Rituals, and Practices of Freedom. Hypatia.

Touchstone, B. (1972). Voodoo in new Orleans. Louisiana History: The Journal of the Louisiana Historical Association